ALAN I W FRANK HOUSE

In Loving Memory of
Mother and Dad

ALAN I W FRANK HOUSE

THE MODERNIST MASTERWORK BY WALTER GROPIUS AND MARCEL BREUER

ESSAYS BY
ALAN I W FRANK
KENNETH FRAMPTON
BARRY BERGDOLL
CHARLES A BIRNBAUM

PRINCIPAL PHOTOGRAPHY BY
EZRA STOLLER AND RICHARD BARNES

IN ASSOCIATION WITH THE
ALAN I W FRANK HOUSE FOUNDATION

RIZZOLI
NEW YORK
New York · Paris · London · Milan

PUBLICATION OF THIS BOOK WAS MADE POSSIBLE IN PART THROUGH THE GENEROUS SUPPORT OF:
HEINZ ENDOWMENTS
RICHARD K MELLON FOUNDATION
PITTSBURGH HISTORY AND LANDMARKS FOUNDATION

First published in the United States of America in 2019 by
Rizzoli International Publications, Inc.
300 Park Avenue South
New York, NY 10010
www.rizzoliusa.com

Texts by Kenneth Frampton, Alan I W Frank, Barry Bergdoll, and Charles A Birnbaum

Photography by Ezra Stoller, Richard Barnes, Richard Pare, and Alan I W Frank

Photographs and essays provided by Alan I W Frank and the Alan I W Frank House Foundation and used with permission. Further credits on page 254.

"New Ways in the New World" © Barry Bergdoll. First published in HÄUSER Magazine 1/2009, Gruner+Jahr GmbH, Hamburg/Germany.

Publisher: Charles Miers
Production Manager: Colin Hough Trapp
Managing Editor: Lynn Scrabis

2019 2020 2021 2022 / 10 9 8 7 6 5 4 3 2 1

ISBN: 978-0-8478-6368-6

Library of Congress Control Number: 2019940360

The Alan I W Frank House, photographed from the front shortly after completion. Four generations of the family of industrialist Robert Frank and his wife Cecelia have lived in this 19,000-square-foot masterwork. It was designed as a complete work of art—landscape, house and interior—by Walter Gropius and Marcel Breuer, and built in Pittsburgh in 1939–40.

Ezra Stoller, 1940

INTRODUCTION

Every day, everywhere we go in our daily lives, we are surrounded by the legacy of an idea begun a hundred years ago in Germany, formed in the imagination of an architect named Walter Gropius, in a school called the Bauhaus. That idea was Modernism, and you can see its influence all around you: in our public spaces, our schools, our office buildings and their interiors, and the furnishings and designs in our homes. All of these things bathe us, visually and physically, in the work of this movement that literally changed every aspect of what was to become modern culture.

Modernism is one of the most important movements in architecture and design in human history. It swept aside old forms of design with a new generation of creative thinking based on truth and new materials such as steel, concrete and new forms of glass. Modernism was more than a new aesthetic; it was a marriage of form and function that connected buildings and the people in them to the earth, air and sky in ways that had not been possible before.

Today, the influence of modernism is so pervasive, so direct and so ubiquitous that it's nearly invisible to the casual observer . . . unless there's a place where one can step back, filter out the noise and be embraced by modernism in a pure and ideal form, on a uniquely human scale, in a setting as treasured and intimate as a grand family home.

There is such a place: the Alan I W Frank House.

It is a family home, and it is built on a grand scale, designed by Gropius himself and one of his most promising students, Marcel Breuer, for a prominent, optimistic Pittsburgh family during the Great Depression. It is the largest and most comprehensive residence Gropius designed, and the only one whose complete interior and furnishings were designed by Breuer. It still stands today, virtually untouched and unchanged, nestled among the oaks and maples of a culturally and intellectually vibrant city neighborhood.

A GREAT LEAP FOR MODERNISM

The architecture of the Frank House expresses the great leap that modernism took when Walter Gropius and Marcel Breuer left 1930s Germany to bring their ideas, their imagination, and their teachings to America. Unlike previous modernist designs in Germany, where a sharp, machined aesthetic defined a rigorous geometric approach, the Frank House achieves a sensuous warmth through gently sculptured curves and warm pink-buff natural stone. The home's soaring expanses of glass and its sensitive rapport with its surrounding grounds suggest a belief in the power of light and environment to nurture the health of body, mind, and spirit. Throughout the interior, the Franks' repeated requests in letters to Gropius and Breuer for "a warm and friendly feeling" to support an active family, social and cultural life, are echoed in the designers' exploration of new materials and warm color palettes.

A MAJOR MONUMENT OF AMERICAN ARCHITECTURAL ART AND HISTORY

Four generations of the family of industrialist Robert Frank and his wife Cecelia have lived in this 19,000-square-foot masterpiece designed as a complete work of art—landscape, interior and furnishings—by Gropius and Breuer, and built in 1939–40. The house, its interior, and its furnishings down to lighting fixtures and fabrics have been lovingly preserved by Cecelia and Robert's youngest child, Alan I W Frank. The house is virtually unchanged since the day the family moved in.

Scholars and critics who have visited the Frank House and seen its intact details and furnishings are unanimous in their understanding of its importance as a masterpiece that must be preserved. J. Carter Brown, former director of the National Gallery of Art in Washington, and considered the country's unofficial minister of culture, described the house as "The Nation's Crown Jewel." Toshiko Mori, former Chair of the Department of Architecture at Harvard University's Graduate School of Design, said the experience of visiting the Frank House is

> *"one of those rare occasions when you enter a house and it's absolutely authentic. Mr. Frank preserved the house in its totality—equipment, furniture, fixtures, even original textiles and wall coverings. It's all intact. It's a very exquisite balance of architectural proportions, textures and colorations with machine-age aesthetics. Everything is very functional."*

A RARE TIME CAPSULE

Like other preserved masterpieces of American architecture, the Frank House is an exquisitely detailed snapshot of a unique point in American history. It documents a time when the restless energy of Pittsburgh's industrial economy found expression in an art form both personal and universal: a cherished family home. And the time it expressed—the sliver of hope between the waning Depression and the looming global war—was one of asserted courage and optimism, framed in the soaring and timeless lines drawn by two of history's greatest architects.

YOU'RE INVITED TO SHARE IN THIS TREASURE

Though years have passed, memories of family, friends, and guests still warm the Frank House. This book brings the joy and hospitality to life through historic and new photography that evokes the warm glow and passion for living that the designers and owners infused in this home.

The book also shares the importance of the home's design and grounds through the words of some of modernism's most respected interpreters: Kenneth Frampton, Ware Professor at the Graduate School of Architecture, Planning and Preservation, Columbia University; Barry Bergdoll, Meyer Schapiro Professor of art history in the Department of Art History and Archaeology at Columbia University; and Charles Birnbaum, FASLA, FAAR, president, CEO, and founder of The Cultural Landscape Foundation. Perhaps most compelling is a walk through the home itself, illuminated by lives lived fully in its soft golden light, written by Alan I W Frank.

THE ORIGIN OF THE FRANK NAME

The Frank name has been part of Pittsburgh's industrial history through four generations of engineers and inventors, reaching back to the birth of American glass and steel in the mid-1800s. It's an ancient name that harkens back to medieval Germany and France. It gave France its name. During serfdom, the name came to be used to mean free, open-hearted, and generous, deriving from the fact that the Franks enjoyed the status of fully free men.

RIGHT: Cecelia Frank's passion for life was the inspiration for the Frank House. She was known to friends as Cele. Here, photographed in 1946, she is standing on a terrace in the back yard by a cherished pear tree that she rescued several times from lightning strikes.

Alan I W Frank, 1946

"I must confess that I am deeply in love with the whole project and that I expect the house to be very noble in appearance."

WALTER GROPIUS

A PHOTOGRAPHIC ESSAY

The home faces East Woodland Road in Pittsburgh's Shadyside neighborhood. Its picturesque approach road is dotted with oaks and maples, and invites visitors to explore the sweeps and curves of stairways and rooms they will encounter when they enter the home.

Richard Pare, 2007

Large shade trees, some centuries old, are a part of the house, connecting it with nature and providing privacy. The large oak at the center of this photo embraces the front terrace.

Richard Barnes, 2008

LEFT: At the front entrance, the visitor is greeted with steel, concrete and glass. Hints of the house's role in the evolution of modernism show in its curves and connection with the landscape.

Ezra Stoller, 1940

RIGHT: Landscape and interior mingle in the ground floor entry, with flagstone flooring, a rubble stone wall and interior plantings. A lobby bench floats on Breuer's Lucite legs.

Ezra Stoller, 1940

RIGHT: Translucent panels illuminate the stairway to the second floor with light from the adjacent recreation room. The sweeping, curling bannister draws the visitor upward, around and into the expanse above.

Richard Barnes, 2008

RIGHT: Space explodes at the top of the stair from the ground floor into a grand reception hall that offers a view of the massive red oak outside, the soaring sculptured main staircase, and a pearwood-paneled bar.

Richard Pare, 2008

RIGHT: The reception hall gives visitors their first full view of the Marcel Breuer furniture that fills every room with curved shapes and soft, natural surfaces trimmed in warm pearwood and English sycamore. Breuer, the 20th century's most influential furniture designer, created every piece specifically for the Frank House, and it is recognized as his best work.

Richard Barnes, 2008

LEFT: The Breuer-designed sofa nestles softly in the curving stairway. For the strength of the stair, Robert Frank used the highest quality steel: Copperweld, made in his own plant in Glassport, Pennsylvania.

Richard Barnes, 2008

RIGHT: Floor-length curtains and sliding glass doors define the home's living spaces. And when it's time for a birthday or Christmas party, they can be pulled back to reveal holiday decorations, setting the stage for surprise and fun.

Ezra Stoller, 1940

LEFT: Lighted makeup mirrors and Breuer-designed stools make the cloakroom a welcome stop before dinner.

Ezra Stoller, 1940

RIGHT: A wooden venetian blind frames the view of the paneled bar. The Swedish crystal was selected by Cele, Robert and the architects.

Ezra Stoller, 1940

LEFT: Viewed from the dining room, the sculptured form of the floating stairway's gently curving shapes provides a dramatic backdrop for social gatherings.

Ezra Stoller, 1940

RIGHT: In the dining room, pearwood tables, floating on Lucite legs, can be configured to seat twenty-four. Instead of traditional chandeliers, ceiling spotlights keep the focus on the table. When desired, the carpet rolls up to reveal an oak parquet dance floor.

Ezra Stoller, 1940

LEFT: All of the Breuer-designed furniture, including these two dining room chairs, contributes to what architectural critic Kenneth Frampton describes as "the undeniably theatrical sensibility that pervades the house."

Ezra Stoller, 1940

LEFT: A gala dinner in 1942. Robert Frank, center, celebrates the birthday of his mother, Mrs. I W Frank, seated to his right.

Family archive, 1942

LEFT: A very young Alan I W Frank toasts his grandmother on her birthday.

Family archive, 1942

RIGHT: Breakfast can be served in a smaller portion of the dining room, separated from the main area by folding doors.

Ezra Stoller, 1940

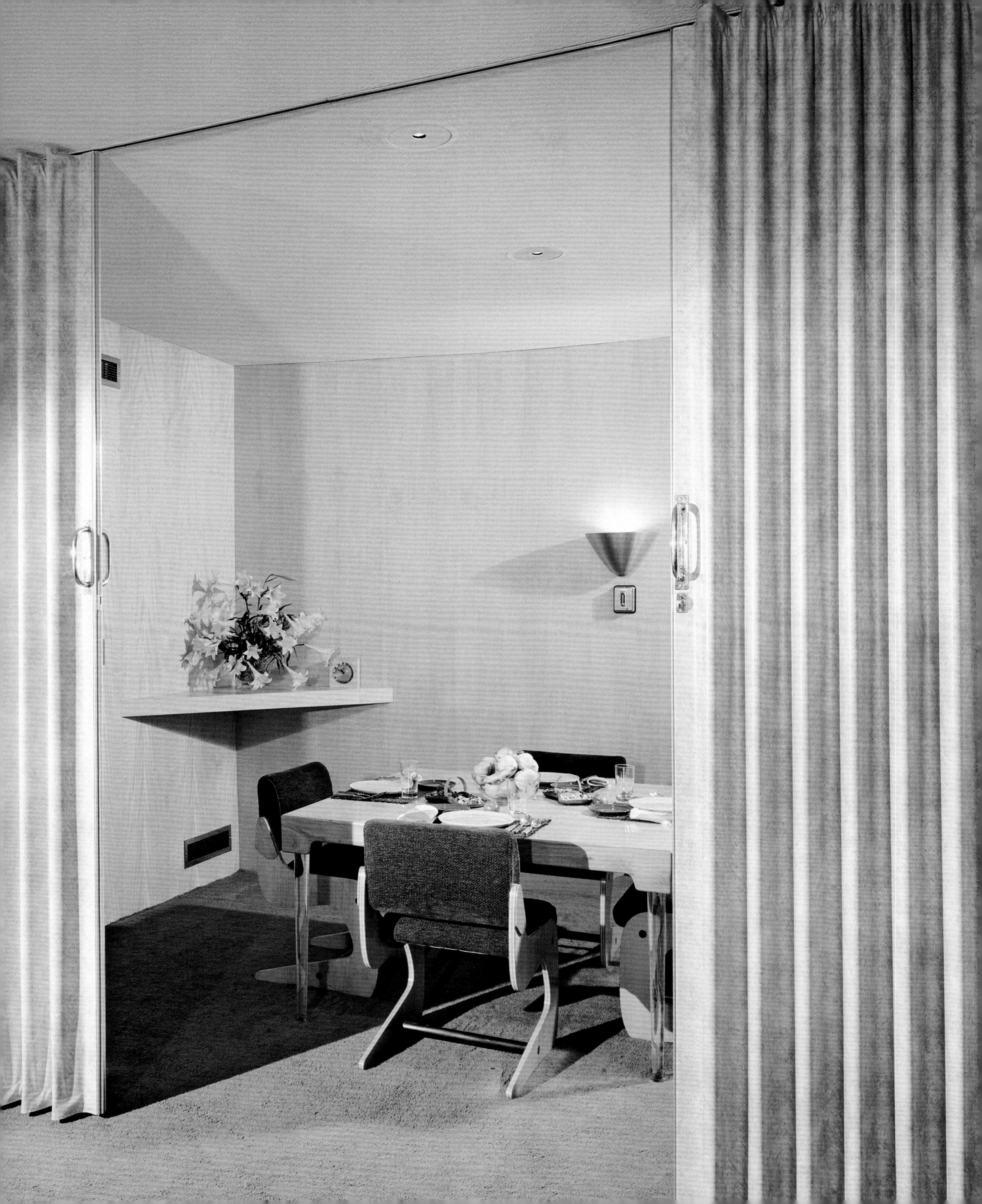

LEFT: Bespoke fixtures designed by Gropius and Breuer exclusively for the Frank House provide warm, indirect illumination throughout the home.

Richard Barnes, 2019

Breuer wanted to leave old, heavy furniture behind for a beautiful new design that appeared light enough to float in space. To accomplish this in his bespoke designs for the Frank House, Breuer called on an exciting new material: duPont Lucite, shown here supporting a pearwood dining room table.

Richard Barnes, 2008

LEFT: Crystal figures and salt dishes capture the afternoon sunshine, infusing it over the warm pearwood surface.

Richard Pare, 2007

RIGHT: Armchairs were designed for the head and foot of the table.

Richard Barnes, 2008

Soft lighting fills the living room (left) and dining room, photographed at night through the large rear windows that face the back terrace.

Ezra Stoller, 1940

The living room and dining room are divided by a freestanding fireplace and chimney, which in the Frank House assumes an unusual aerodynamic form, faced throughout in polished travertine. A heat management system invented by Robert Frank automatically adjusts the home's heating and cooling system when the fireplace is in use.

Ezra Stoller, 1940

A rare early color photo highlights living room sofa cushions that can be reversed and arranged in a variety of red, blue and chocolate brown patterns.

Ezra Stoller, 1940

LEFT: A sunny corner of the living room is home to a Breuer pearwood card table with leather inlaid top.

Richard Barnes, 2019

RIGHT: Removing the card table's top reveals a beautiful inlaid leather backgammon surface. The top itself, when reversed, is an inlaid wood checkerboard.

Richard Barnes, 2019

The warm, inviting study features a Breuer chaise longue, desk and sofa. The dominant furniture covering in the room is a brown fabric with silver thread. It, along with the zebra sofa cushions, was designed for the house by Anni Albers. The conservatory at the rear of the photo, equally visible from both the living and dining spaces, helps tie them together.

Ezra Stoller, 1940

RIGHT: A view from outside the study reveals a large collection of books on architecture and modern art from the 1930s, with focused reading lamps.

Ezra Stoller, 1940

AMERICA
THE WAVERLEY NOVELS
KENILWORTH
FAIR MAID OF PERTH
GUY MANNERING
REDGAUNTLET
THE HEART OF MIDLOTHIAN
CASTLE DANGEROUS
GLOSSARY
THE PIRATE
ST RONAN'S WELL
TALES OF A GRANDFATHER
ROB ROY
OLD MORTALITY
IVANHOE
THE TALISMAN
THE MONASTERY
THE ABBOT
ROUTLEDGE
ceiling s
ceiling n
ON
porch
conservatory
conservatory
conservatory plugs
plugs
OFF

LEFT: The study's pearwood bookshelf frames a view of the living room and the stairway beyond.

Richard Pare, 2007

RIGHT: Inventor and industrialist Robert Frank insisted on the latest technology throughout the house. In 1940, this meant silent mercury light switches, conduit wiring, and circuit breakers instead of fuses.

Ezra Stoller, 1940

THE FIRST WORLD WAR
EDITED BY LAURENCE STALLINGS
REMBRANDT: COMPLETE ETCHINGS
LETTERS TO EMILE BERNARD
Leaves of Grass
FANTASTIC ART DADA SURREALISM
THE MUSEUM OF MODERN ART
Photography
A SHORT CRITICAL HISTORY

LEFT: The Frank House is the home of Marcel Breuer's first floating, cantilevered stairway. With soaring lines and seemingly weightless strength, this design would become the signature feature of Breuer's architecture.

Richard Barnes, 2008

RIGHT: The stairway is a shaped and sculptured connection between the interior of the house and the outside world that embraces it. Pressed against the home's two-story curved window, the stairway leads the visitor out into a landscape of trees, sky, and seasons, while holding fast to the warm, comforting interior.

Richard Barnes, 2010

LEFT: The technology that defies gravity: concrete reinforced with chrome-finished, copper-covered steel bars from Robert Frank's Copperweld steel mill.

Ezra Stoller, 1940

RIGHT: Atop the stairway is a spacious sitting room that connects a large terrace with the family bedrooms and a guest room.

Richard Barnes, 2008

RIGHT: The second-floor sitting room overlooks a spacious sun-dappled terrace and the centuries-old red oak shade tree that embraces it.

Richard Pare, 2008

A granite fireplace and chimney form the centerpiece of the second-floor sitting room. With bedrooms and guest rooms communicating with this social space, it is designed to accommodate breakfast when guests visit, served from a hot cart via the elevator.

Ezra Stoller, 1940

LEFT: The second-floor sitting room's built-in bookshelves include a mailbox slot for each family member.

Ezra Stoller, 1940

RIGHT: One of the first aspects of American home design that caught the eye of Walter Gropius was New England clapboard siding. In the Frank House, Gropius and Breuer turned clapboard 90 degrees, expressing it with vertical laps of pearwood.

Alan I W Frank, 2019

LEFT: Bold, simple geometries coupled with comfortable form characterize a bespoke Breuer armchair designed for the second-floor sitting room.

Ezra Stoller, 1940

LEFT: Curios from generations of family adventures overlook a Breuer original sofa with built-in cabinets in the second-floor sitting room.

Ezra Stoller, 1940

RIGHT: Cowhide adds a rustic touch to the natural warmth of a pearwood armchair, accented by a background cactus plant.

Ezra Stoller, 1940

RIGHT: The second-floor breakfast table rests on legs joined by horizontal grillwork.

Ezra Stoller, 1940

RIGHT: The warmth of pearwood supporting the second-floor breakfast table complements a display of antique bottles, an early example of the Frank family's industrial presence in Western Pennsylvania.

Richard Barnes, 2019

Breuer armchairs, night table, desk and chair grace a second-floor bedroom.

Ezra Stoller, 1940

Breuer reveled in the use of innovative materials, including cork as a covering for walls and ceilings. The Franks shared his enthusiasm, and applauded its use in their son Alan's bathroom (right).

ABOVE: *Alan I W Frank, 2019*
RIGHT: *Ezra Stoller, 1940*

LAVORIS
HAIR TONIC

LEFT: Shelves, racks and other built-in amenities provide a place for everything.

Ezra Stoller, 1940

RIGHT: Breuer created bedrooms that are entered through a curved pathway that both draws the visitor in and defines a unique interior world.

Richard Barnes, 2019

RIGHT: Breuer hallmarks adorn every private room—indirect lighting, subtle wall textures, curtains, and warm, relaxing chairs.

Richard Pare, 2007

LEFT: Kimberly's room includes a desk with built-in shelves and adjoining bathroom.

Richard Pare, 2007

HI, SWEETIE!
THE ELLIS SCHOOL
A SWIFTLY TILTING PLANET
MADELEINE L'ENGLE
NORMAN VINCENT PEALE
BIBLE STORIES
BIBLE
A Love Story
by Erich Beagle
GIVENCHY

LEFT: Kimberly's desk includes built-in space for favorite things.

Richard Barnes, 2019

RIGHT: Kimberly's bath features a dressing table lit from below. Different lighting options can be set for daylight and evening.

Richard Barnes, 2019

LEFT: Bath closet has carefully organized built-in shelves of warm pearwood.

Richard Pare, 2007

LEFT: A skylight illuminates the corridor to the master bedroom.

Richard Barnes, 2019

The master bedroom connects with its own large private terrace. The pearwood night tables were drawn by Florence Knoll while she worked as a draftsperson for Gropius and Breuer in Cambridge. She eventually went on to found, with partner and husband Hans Knoll, Knoll Associates—the firm that gave the mid-century American office interior its distinctive modern look.

Ezra Stoller, 1940

RIGHT: The glass block floor of the master terrace passes diffused sunlight through to the space below.

Ezra Stoller, 1940

LEFT: The master bedroom's wall fabric, woven with copper thread, is by Anni Albers, as are many of the fabrics in the house. In the fireplace, framed in Italian marble and connected by flagstone to the terrace, a cozy fire warms the room.

Richard Barnes, 2019

. . . And Thy Neighbor
SAM SHOEMAKER
talks about creative living
Offill

LEFT: In the master bedroom, innovative reading lamps focus a small spot of light just where it's needed. These fixtures were a predecessor to airline reading lights.

Richard Barnes, 2019

RIGHT: Off the master bedroom, Cele's bath connects with a dressing room paneled in English sycamore.

Richard Barnes, 2019

LEFT: Bathroom walls are deep burgundy Carrara glass topped by a translucent layer that brings light in from the dressing room beyond. The marble floor is kept warm in the winter by hot water circulating under it.

Richard Barnes, 2019

RIGHT: Cele's dressing room is paneled in English sycamore, with Breuer chairs and Lucite drawer handles.

Ezra Stoller, 1940

LEFT: Wrapping around the bath, the spacious dressing room offers the comfort of Breuer lounge chairs, a full-length dressing table and desk, and a convenient built-in scale.

Richard Barnes, 2019

A chaise longue covered in deep red fabric offers a quiet spot to relax.

Richard Barnes, 2019

A wall-mounted folding mirror marks the exit from Cele's dressing room to the hallway.

Richard Barnes, 2019

ABOVE: Robert Frank's original file folder for Gropius and Breuer, with Breuer's four-digit home phone number.

Family archives, 1939

LEFT: Robert's dressing room includes a Breuer desk and chair.

Ezra Stoller, 1940

RIGHT: Robert's bathroom features a pull-down scale (left), wall-mounted hair dryer (upper right) and shoe polisher (lower right).

Ezra Stoller, 1940

LEFT: The entry to the guest room is flanked by the elevator and a refreshment bar with small cooler.

Richard Barnes, 2008

RIGHT: Breuer's Lucite door handles are ergonomic as well as attractive. In addition, they pass light through from the other side, making them easy to find in the dark.

Richard Barnes, 2019

The guest room is designed with table and bath.

Ezra Stoller, 1940

RIGHT: Fabric with a Native American pattern covers the guest room wall.

Richard Barnes, 2019

In spring, the front entry is embraced by rhododendron blossoms.

Alan I W Frank, 2010

RIGHT: Spring foliage envelops the stairway outside the pool's glass wall.

Richard Barnes, 2008

RIGHT: With its glass wall open to the warm weather, the indoor pool connects to the patio and stairway.

Ezra Stoller, 1940

The pool, with a sliding glass wall, provides year-round enjoyment and a spectacular view of the landscape.

Ezra Stoller, 1940

RIGHT: Just next to the pool, the ground floor recreation room offers a place for refreshment and relaxation.

Ezra Stoller, 1940

RIGHT: The recreation room's bar combines cool drinks with freeform sculpture.

Ezra Stoller, 1940

RIGHT: Long horizontal windows with venetian blinds open to the front of the house.

Ezra Stoller, 1940

An important part of the recreation room is its rubble stone fireplace. On the opposite wall, translucent windows pass light through to the stairway. On the back wall, a small door below the light fixture opens for projecting movies. Breuer chairs and floor cushions trimmed in cowhide set the mood for fun.

Ezra Stoller, 1940

A large terrace over the indoor pool opens to the outdoors on three sides, including this view of the Breuer-designed back yard with its freeform pond, stone walls, and flowing landscape.

Ezra Stoller, 1940

RIGHT: Soaring above the open terrace, a second-floor deck brings daylight in through its glass floor.

Ezra Stoller, 1940

Steps from the first floor terrace blend into a freeform network of flagstones that unite the landscape and its features with the house.

Ezra Stoller, 1940

Sloping terrain, typical of Western Pennsylvania, flows from the back of the house over a series of terraces and walls. An awning shades the second-floor master terrace from the summer sun.

Ezra Stoller, 1940

The separate garage, built into the hillside, has a grass roof. It includes an indoor shooting range.

Ezra Stoller, 1940

Every spring, Cele's flowers, including these wisteria blossoms, start their spectacular parade of color and delight.

Alan I W Frank, 2010

Magnolia blossoms embrace the house.

Alan I W Frank, 2010

White peonies fill the lawn with the look of summer.

Alan I W Frank, 2010

Inside the house as I was showing our guest our home, I assured her that it was safe to climb the rest of the stairs to the second floor. Probably less because of the confidence of a young boy than the lack of a viable alternative, she made it to the top.

There we stepped into a wonderful living space that has nurtured our family's life together, from my childhood to that of my children and grandchildren—our second-floor family room.

That room, like all the other parts of our home, is virtually unchanged since that sunny day in 1940. Now as then, as you enter from the top of the cantilevered stair, a large granite fireplace provides warmth and stability, with pillows scattered on the floor in front. On the other side, large windows bring the outside in, and a door opens to a terrace nestled in the upper branches of the large red oak. Over a comfortable Breuer-designed sofa at one end of the room are blue-turquoise glass bottles my great-grandfather made in Pittsburgh in the 1860s and sea shells my children found on our trips to far-away islands.

At the other end is a refreshment bar with a compartment to keep food and drinks cool. The cooler is silent because it, together with other coolers in the house, is powered by a 1940 Frigidaire compressor on the ground floor that is still working faithfully. My parents wanted the living areas of the house to be quiet, so equipment is located two floors below and even the heavy-wall copper piping connecting it is wrapped in sound-absorbent insulation.

The pearwood walls infuse the room with beautiful warm tan and brown hues. Gropius and Breuer saw New England clapboard when they came to the United States, and liked its look. On one long wall in this room, they turned it ninety degrees, making pearwood panels that overlap vertically. Bookshelves made of the same wood were built in front. It is here that the family listened on December 8, 1941, to Franklin Delano Roosevelt's speech describing the attack on Pearl Harbor, with a cream-colored leather-covered Liberty radio that still sits on the pearwood table Breuer designed for it.

Mother and Dad wanted our guests to be able to wake up and have breakfast whenever they wanted. To make that possible, the four sculptural pearwood and leather chairs that usually rest along the upper curve of the staircase were moved to a table in front of a long window facing the front yard. Then Jimmy, whom we considered part of the family and who ran the house for Mother and then me for more than half a century, brought the hot-cold wagon up from the kitchen in the elevator and wheeled it to the area where the chairs had been. The delicious breakfast he had prepared waited in hot and cold compartments of the wagon at just the right temperatures until our guests came out of the guestroom and were ready to eat.

I always thought that the stainless-steel hot-cold wagon was designed by Gropius and Breuer, as was almost everything else in the house, until recently when I was looking at the drawing for it and I saw the initials at the bottom. They were Dad's.

ABOVE: The second-floor sitting room was a favorite area for everyone to relax, with cushions on the floor in front of the granite fireplace, across from the magnificent curved window.

Ezra Stoller, 1940

RIGHT: The master bedroom. Reading lights are specially designed to project a small beam of light that enables one person to read without disturbing anyone nearby. They are a predecessor of reading lights in aircraft.

Richard Barnes, 2019

White peonies fill the lawn with the look of summer.

Alan I W Frank, 2010

A WALK THROUGH THE HOUSE BY ALAN I W FRANK

The sun bounced playful highlights on her light brown hair as she climbed the gently curving staircase. She was looking to her right, out the two-story bay window cradled by a centuries-old oak. Suddenly she stopped. Her gaze shifted from the magnificent oak downward, and she could not see anything holding up the steps on which she was standing.

She had never been on a stair that seemed to be floating in air. It was a beautiful piece of sculpture, Marcel Breuer's brilliant cantilevered stairway in our new home.

I was a very young boy and I was performing one of my first jobs, showing a friend of my mother and dad our house. There was so much new and exciting about it.

"Alan I W Frank should know what it's like to live in a Bauhaus property better than anyone. He's lived in one almost his whole life."

NEW YORK TIMES
APRIL 18, 2019

I remember, a little more than a year before, my parents bringing me here for the first time. Standing on the hillside, I had been fascinated by the big yellow machine scooping up the top layer of earth and I saw for the first time the dark brown fertile soil below, then layers of reddish-brown shale, and beneath it all solid rock. Soon this would become a curve of our driveway, inviting people in, with a native stone retaining wall on one side and, on the other, a carpet of grass underlying splendid pink dogwood trees.

A couple hundred feet away, other machines were making an enormous hole, all the larger from my youthful perspective, that would become the swimming pool. Huge steel girders were being welded into place and concrete trucks were arriving and what seemed to be an endless stream of men and wheelbarrows were taking the fresh concrete over wood boards and pouring it into wooden forms to create the floors and walls of our home.

It was 1939 and World War II had broken out in Europe. Some observers, looking at the steel structure of the house, thought a ship was being built. The garage was separate, set deeply into a hillside, with grass on top and three sides. A few wondered if it was a secret aircraft hangar.

Dad, who was a peaceful man, thought that if war did come to the United States, we should be prepared. The garage contains a shooting range. Among the many targets, there was an enemy parachutist floating down.

LEFT: Alan I W Frank

Kimberly Frank Shaw, 1980

RIGHT: Alan's sister Barbara, Walter Gropius, and Alan watch construction. Heavy steel I-beams have been welded in place to form the structure of the house.

Robert Frank, 1939

Inside the house as I was showing our guest our home, I assured her that it was safe to climb the rest of the stairs to the second floor. Probably less because of the confidence of a young boy than the lack of a viable alternative, she made it to the top.

There we stepped into a wonderful living space that has nurtured our family's life together, from my childhood to that of my children and grandchildren—our second-floor family room.

That room, like all the other parts of our home, is virtually unchanged since that sunny day in 1940. Now as then, as you enter from the top of the cantilevered stair, a large granite fireplace provides warmth and stability, with pillows scattered on the floor in front. On the other side, large windows bring the outside in, and a door opens to a terrace nestled in the upper branches of the large red oak. Over a comfortable Breuer-designed sofa at one end of the room are blue-turquoise glass bottles my great-grandfather made in Pittsburgh in the 1860s and sea shells my children found on our trips to far-away islands.

At the other end is a refreshment bar with a compartment to keep food and drinks cool. The cooler is silent because it, together with other coolers in the house, is powered by a 1940 Frigidaire compressor on the ground floor that is still working faithfully. My parents wanted the living areas of the house to be quiet, so equipment is located two floors below and even the heavy-wall copper piping connecting it is wrapped in sound-absorbent insulation.

The pearwood walls infuse the room with beautiful warm tan and brown hues. Gropius and Breuer saw New England clapboard when they came to the United States, and liked its look. On one long wall in this room, they turned it ninety degrees, making pearwood panels that overlap vertically. Bookshelves made of the same wood were built in front. It is here that the family listened on December 8, 1941, to Franklin Delano Roosevelt's speech describing the attack on Pearl Harbor, with a cream-colored leather-covered Liberty radio that still sits on the pearwood table Breuer designed for it.

Mother and Dad wanted our guests to be able to wake up and have breakfast whenever they wanted. To make that possible, the four sculptural pearwood and leather chairs that usually rest along the upper curve of the staircase were moved to a table in front of a long window facing the front yard. Then Jimmy, whom we considered part of the family and who ran the house for Mother and then me for more than half a century, brought the hot-cold wagon up from the kitchen in the elevator and wheeled it to the area where the chairs had been. The delicious breakfast he had prepared waited in hot and cold compartments of the wagon at just the right temperatures until our guests came out of the guestroom and were ready to eat.

I always thought that the stainless-steel hot-cold wagon was designed by Gropius and Breuer, as was almost everything else in the house, until recently when I was looking at the drawing for it and I saw the initials at the bottom. They were Dad's.

ABOVE: The second-floor sitting room was a favorite area for everyone to relax, with cushions on the floor in front of the granite fireplace, across from the magnificent curved window.

Ezra Stoller, 1940

RIGHT: The master bedroom. Reading lights are specially designed to project a small beam of light that enables one person to read without disturbing anyone nearby. They are a predecessor of reading lights in aircraft.

Richard Barnes, 2019

This special room was also the setting for a happy childhood lived by me and my two sisters, with plenty of fun and laughter. When my sister Barbara, eight years my senior, started going out on dates, I thought it would be great fun to play a trick on her. In the workshop, I fastened a battery and a bell to a board, with a simple switch I made by bending a piece of metal. I strung a string across the top stair just before the second floor, and when Barbara came home from her date that night and came up the stair, her foot moved the string and the bell started ringing. I thought it was hilarious. Fortunately, after her initial shock, my sister's sense of humor replaced surprise and we had a good laugh together.

A few weeks later, expecting that she would be on the lookout for the string, I set up an invisible infrared beam. Again, success. Little brother could retire from playing tricks on his beloved older sister. This was also a relief to my other sister, Joan, who is six years older than me. Growing up, Joan developed a passion for the arts and has continued my mother's work for Pittsburgh's music and theater organizations.

This wonderful family space opens to the family bedrooms and the guest bedroom. A few steps through the gentle curve of the entrance to my bedroom takes us into my special world.

The walls are paneled in maple. The bed is upholstered in brown leather. A second brown leather bed is set in a niche across the room, topped with rectilinear pillows so that it looks like a couch. A handsome Breuer desk, desk chair, two other chairs, built-in bookcase, and cabinet complete the room. It is fun and happy, and just the right size to feel comfortable.

The bathroom walls, ceiling, and floor are cork. Built into the walls are a scale, a hairdryer, and a cabinet to shine shoes. The closet has shelves and compartments for shirts, coats, socks, shoes, and everything else.

Sometimes I took our guests into my parents' bedroom with its large windows and terrace overlooking a portion of two acres of garden, rubble walls, and fish pond where rabbits, squirrels, birds, and deer make their home. Anni Albers, renowned twentieth-century fabric designer, created the wall fabric, which has a copper thread running through it. The fireplace is made of red marble from Italy.

Mother's bathroom walls are deep burgundy Carrara glass and the marble floor is kept warm in the winter by hot water circulating under it. Her dressing room is paneled in English sycamore.

Dad's dressing room, next door, is redwood and grass cloth, and his bathroom and large walk-in shower are cork.

What is now my daughter Kimberly's bedroom is one of my favorites. It has the largest bed in the house, cradled in a gently curving wall covered in handsome tan textured fabric. It also includes a pearwood desk and pearwood bookcase, which in addition to books, holds hundreds of seashells Kim collected from faraway islands, a desk chair, an arm chair, and two tables. It is intimate, nurturing, and stunning.

Her bathroom is a few steps away, with walls of warm cream-colored Carrara glass. It includes a dressing table and chair and opens to the closet, which has built-in places for all her clothes.

Two other bedrooms and baths, an elevator, front terrace, and a maid's room complete the second floor.

These second-floor bedrooms, and the family space that adjoins them, form a seamless home within the home, intended by its designers to encourage and nurture family life. Each room in the house has its own palette of harmonious colors, and the next room embodies its own subtly different palette. From room to room, the colors flow like a beautiful symphony.

One day my ten-year-old granddaughter Susanne, who was sitting on the bed in Kimberly's bedroom, said, "I love this house and this bedroom. Everything is perfect. The bed is just the right height, the night table is right here with the radio and stuffed animals. And there is a built-in shelf on the other side holding the telephone and the other things I need. Everything is where it should be, and it is all so beautiful."

In that moment, without anyone ever explaining it to her, Susanne understood the house. She appreciated perfectly what Mother and Dad and Gropius and Breuer wanted to create.

It is fascinating to read the hundreds of letters between Mother and Dad, and Gropius and Breuer. In one, Dad said he thought that the maid's room was too small. The architects wrote back that to make it bigger they would have to increase the spacing of the steel structure, making the whole house larger. He told them to just take space out of his dressing room, and that is what was done. My parents wanted everyone working for them to be content.

In good weather, I take our guests from the second floor up to the roof deck, which has an area for dancing and overlooks much of the city. The third floor also has two bedrooms, the thirteenth bathroom in the house, and a storage room. Initially it housed our cook, who came from Sweden, and twin seventeen-year-old girls from Norway who worked as housemaids. Sixty-five years later, the daughter of one of them came by to say hello after attending her daughter's college graduation.

Sometimes my tour starts on the ground floor after guests have come up the curving drive to the front door. They come in through the front entrance filled with plants and then enter the recreation room. They see the piano, sized so that it can fit in the elevator and be taken up to the first floor for parties; and then the Capehart radio phonograph, built into a cabinet along the wall to provide music for the recreation room, pool, and living room. It was the first

machine that could play a record on one side, turn it over and play the other side, and then go on to the next record.

Alongside the Capehart is a pony-skin sofa and large rubble stone fireplace with pillows scattered on the floor in front, along with a ping-pong table and a refreshment bar with Breuer-designed bar stools. Opposite the bar, doors open to a storage room and a wine cellar.

At one end of the recreation room is the projection room, where I showed 16-millimeter movies—on film that had a soundtrack—on a pull-down screen at the other end of the room. I also used the projection room as my photography darkroom.

Sometimes this room was used for other purposes besides play, ping-pong, music and movies. I remember on one of my birthdays when my whole class and other friends came over, Jimmy set up dinner tables for us in the recreation room.

And beyond the recreation room beckons the seductive beauty of the swimming pool some have called the most romantic in the world.

The pool has a remarkably strong gravitational pull on those who come near. Otherwise sane humans have been known to spontaneously dive in. Thousands of happy voices have acclaimed it over the years as the most fun part of the house.

One wall of the pool room is all glass and in warm weather can slide back to open onto a flagstone terrace. In the wintertime, with mist rising from the warm blue water, and snow outside, it is truly magical.

The pool is twenty feet wide and forty feet long, and has three dressing rooms. Mother and Dad wanted the pool not only for enjoyment but for a healthy lifestyle. That was an important objective for them and the architects.

At the other end of the recreation room is the workroom. It still has Dad's tools, wood and metalworking equipment, and an electric furnace that can melt copper and bronze. It holds my large standard-gauge train set on a platform that folds down and covers most of the room, and a radio-controlled airplane Dad and I built in the 1940s. And it contains a working steam engine my grandfather I W built when he was thirteen by making sand molds for each piece, pouring molten bronze into each mold, and then machining each part. Later in his life he engineered and built much of the machinery that went into the creation of the steel industry that began in Pittsburgh and helped build industrial America in the twentieth century.

A wood cellar, another storage room, dog kennel, boiler room, and air-conditioning room with equipment to clean the air and control temperature and humidity complete the ground floor. Most of the equipment is original and still working well. For example, the main

LEFT: Kimberly's bedroom. Intimate, nurturing and stunning.

Richard Pare, 2007

ABOVE: Swimming pool.

Ezra Stoller, 1940

SCENES FROM CHILDHOOD BIRTHDAYS

Kimberly and Darcy Frank — Alan's daughters

Don "Chef" Brockett, a character from *Mr Rogers' Neighborhood* (and a neighbor), brings Kimberly her birthday cake.

Darcy opens her birthday presents.

A BIRTHDAY SURPRISE

My home was an important part of a wonderful childhood for me and my friends and classmates. My birthday parties were the best. I invited everyone in my class, and we played and swam in the pool, and then had dinner.

Once when it was time for ice cream and cake, we were all sitting at the dining room table and in walked Chef Brockett from *Mr Rogers' Neighborhood*! Everyone's jaw dropped at the surprise. It was one of so many wonderful parties we had, but it is definitely the one no one will ever forget. — Kimberly Frank Shaw

Kimberly and friends splash in the pool.

Kimberly playing piano.

Alan I W Frank, 1970s

On Darcy's birthday, Chef Brockett serves the birthday cake.

Darcy creating a musical composition.

Fleming, part of the family for over half a century, brings Kimberly's birthday cake to her.

Kimberly hugging her donkey.

Alan I W Frank, 1970s

Alan and his daughters.

Town & Country
Used with permission of
Hearst Magazine Media

air handler is a five-foot 1940 Buffalo Forge fan powered by a 1940 Westinghouse two-horsepower electric motor, running smoothly and quietly. And the refrigerators throughout the house are kept cool by two 1940 Frigidaire compressors.

But guests do not usually see these rooms when they arrive at the ground-floor front entrance. They come up the stairway from the ground floor to the first floor and into the reception area, to be welcomed and embraced by a gently curving travertine wall.

When I stand next to that beautiful travertine sculpture which divides the reception area, the dining room, and the living room, I feel that I am in the embrace of the wings of an angel. To me, it is in plain sight, this beautiful angel twelve feet high, its huge wings providing form and shape, protection and direction.

And across the room is that stunning masterpiece, that most spectacular of stairways, Copperweld steel and concrete floating in air, nestled in a centuries-old oak, on which we began our journey.

This space flows seamlessly into the living room and its travertine fireplace. On Christmas Eve, this is where my children and I would light a fire and wait for Santa to come. My daughters would leave milk and cookies for him here, or sometimes in the next room, the study, when they thought he might come down that chimney.

ABOVE: Cele Frank (right) and friend preparing to depart for the Symphony Ball.

Family archive, 1958

RIGHT: Travertine wall in the first floor reception area. The light fixture was designed by the architects and built by Wendel Lighting to cast light on the ceiling, bathing the room in a soft, gentle glow.

Richard Pare, 2007

Seamless transitions like this are everywhere. All of the rooms on the first floor are designed to flow into each other. Everyone can move easily to mix and mingle and enjoy each other's company. And whether there is one or fifty people in the room, there is an intimacy of design that makes them feel comfortable.

The study is another warm, friendly room, with a tan Kasota stone fireplace on one side and hundreds of books on pearwood shelves on the other. At one end is the conservatory filled with lush planting. Outside, a large terrace open on three sides over the swimming pool looks out to the pond and Breuer's rubble walls and landscape in the backyard. Four doors from the first floor to the outside make it easy to walk to the garden, and are another way, in addition to large windows, the architects made the house and the landscape as one.

ABOVE: A dinner party celebrates the 82nd birthday of Mrs. I W Frank, Alan's grandmother. She and Robert are at the end of the table. Jimmy, who was part of our family for more than half a century, is serving squabs to the guests. The Swedish crystal, plates, and flatware had been selected by Mother and Dad and Gropius and Breuer.

Family archive, 1942

The Kasota stone used to build the study fireplace also covers most of the outside of the house. Huge blocks of this beautiful sandstone were carefully cut from an ancient inland sea in Minnesota that existed about 450 million years ago, and look like a pink sand beach. Many of the pieces of Kasota stone weigh eight hundred pounds each, and are attached with bronze anchors to the heavy steel I-beams that are welded together to form the structure of the house. The galvanized-steel Hope windows are also welded to the steel superstructure. Inside the stone is an air space for insulation, and then a brick wall and the interior walls.

Christmas dinner is always in the dining room on Breuer's elegant pearwood table, floating on Lucite legs. Additional sections of the table can be added to seat twenty-four comfortably. Hidden lights in the ceiling illuminate just to the edge of the table. The carpet can be rolled up to reveal a light oak parquet dance floor. On Christmas a special tablecloth and decorations give everything a special warm, festive mood.

On many occasions, there were more than twenty-four for dinner. My mother invited a steady stream of interesting people from the arts, sciences, and government—the actor

Cecelia Frank will be hostess tonight in her Woodland Road home at a reception-supper party honoring the distinguished actor, Sir John Gielgud.

Sir John is appearing tonight in Carnegie Music Hall in Shakespeare's "Ages of Man".

Among the guests who will attend the theater and the reception-supper party are Mr and Mrs John A Byerly, Mrs Clifford S Heinz, Mrs Robert J Dodds, and Dr William E McEllroy.

PITTSBURGH POST-GAZETTE
DECEMBER 16, 1958

Sir John Gielgud, the ballerina Margot Fonteyn, architects, senators, and friends from all walks of life and circumstances. She believed a person's character was what was important, not where they were from, the color of their skin, or whether they were wealthy. If they tried to make other people's lives better, they could be her friend. Isn't that the way it should be?

One of Mother's good friends was Bill McEllroy. He discovered one of the vitamins when he was in his twenties, and was dean of the medical school of the University of Pittsburgh for many years afterward. He brought in a young researcher, Jonas Salk, and established him in the laboratory, where Salk developed the vaccine that rid the world of polio. Bill McEllroy recruited other outstanding scientists from around the world to take charge of other parts of the Medical Center. He often asked Mother's assistance in doing this, bringing over to our house many of the people he was trying to attract, with the two of them convincing the candidates to move to Pittsburgh to help build the future.

Mother also worked indefatigably to build the musical organizations in this city, in particular the symphony, the civic light opera, and the youth symphony. I was told a few years ago, "Your mother is why the music groups are here."

Another friend, the producer of a number of popular Broadway shows, in many of which Mother owned a share, happened to mention to her one day that the young cast of the show that was in town for the holidays had no place to go for Christmas. Mother said simply, "Bring them over," and so the entire cast and the stagehands joined the family for Christmas dinner.

As I was growing up, each year I had a New Year's Eve party. I invited perhaps fifty or a hundred friends, and many more came. Apparently, this was the place to be. But no matter what, after the last guest departed, Jimmy, Fleming, Hanley, Hilliard, and Estelle, loyal members of the household, without being asked, made sure everything was clean and put back in its place, and then had their own party in their own sitting room.

A bar and cloak room complete the guest area of the first floor. Then comes Hanley's pantry. He had come from England, and when I was a boy I loved to listen to his stories of the "old country." Next is Jimmy's kitchen. Jimmy ordered food chosen by my mother and prepared it. When company came, he arranged what was needed. Often that included a musical group playing in the reception area, living room, or dining room. The kitchen's original 1940 stove and refrigerator are still working quietly and faithfully.

The servant's sitting room is adjacent to the kitchen and pantry. For decades the postman came in, delivering the mail. Jimmy made him a cup of coffee, and they talked. Jimmy knew everything that was happening in the neighborhood. Years later after I graduated from Harvard and served as a Special Agent of the Counter Intelligence Corps, I wished our country had knowledge of what was going on in the world that was as good as Jimmy's knowledge of Pittsburgh.

Among the home's many innovative systems—one that Mother invented—is the light signal, an improvement to our private phone system. If someone wants to communicate with another person in the house, he or she can use one of the private exchange telephones that are in each room to light up the other person's number on a small light blue screen mounted in the wall. A soft musical chime sounds when the number is illuminated, and the person called can answer with the telephone in the room he is in. A switch in each bedroom can turn off the light and chime at night. Everyone in the home had their own number.

Mother was Number One.

In an era when most women did not go to college, she did. At a time when most women did not have a career, she had one. And when women did not have the right to vote, she worked quietly and effectively until they did.

Her family always came first, and she was always first with us. No matter what, she was always there, with "God's love on earth." A brass plaque on the rector's door in our neighborhood church honors her with those words.

Mother was the center of the family. She was the light that inspired each of us in our many different ways, and the center of gravity that held us all together.

Hundreds of letters between Mother and Dad and Gropius and Breuer that are preserved at the house make clear her influence in the important change that took place in architecture when Gropius and Breuer came to the United States.

My parents never allowed much publicity about the house because it was our home, but they did permit one article to be published in Architectural Forum in March 1941. It states:

> *"Many factors combine to emphasize the importance of this house ... Its architects are unquestioned leaders of this phase of the modern movement, Walter Gropius being not only one of its originators, but the only member of the European group who has remained continuously in practice since its inception. Neither Mies van der Rohe, Oud, nor Le Corbusier, for example, has built a single building in the past five years.*
>
> *In its use of random ashlar, stone veneer, travertine and natural wood is indicated a new interest in natural materials. Also worth noting is the disintegration of the rectangle into freer shapes, as in the stairway, garden walls and entrance vestibule. If in so important an example such drastic modifications are to be seen, there is new and impressive evidence that contemporary architecture is entering a new phase, richer, more assured, and more human."*

RIGHT: Cecelia Frank (1900–1971) was the center of the family. She was also the inspiration for, and an active partner in the creation of the Frank House. When she wasn't helping the University of Pittsburgh recruit pioneering doctors to its growing Medical School, Cele was hosting dinners, parties and other events for Pittsburgh's musical, theatrical, cultural and intellectual communities.

Family archive, 1968

Dad was an engineer, as was my grandfather. When I was growing up, on weekends Dad and I made things in the workshop. Often we made something new for the house. I remember when I was nine, we made an electric-powered wagon that I drove around the ground floor. What fun! It was powered by a spare motor for the heat-recycling system Dad designed, which used the heat that the air-conditioning system removed from the house in the summer to heat the pool.

Robert Frank (1898–1965) was an executive with the Copperweld Steel Company, a booming Pittsburgh enterprise. An engineer like his father, Robert possessed an endless curiosity and passion for solutions that bring progress to society—talents he brought to the Frank House. He and Cele collaborated extensively with the architects in the design and layout of the house, and Robert invented many of the innovative systems that manage heating, cooling, and air quality in the home.

Family archive, 1942

WALTER GROPIUS AND MARCEL BREUER
ASSOCIATED ARCHITECTS
1430 MASSACHUSETTS AVENUE
CAMBRIDGE, MASS.
TELEPHONE - KIRKLAND 6088

March 31, 1939.

Robert J. Frank, Esq.
1336 Inverness Avenue
Pittsburgh, Pennsylvania.

Dear Mr. Frank:

After your long telephone call on Wednesday, we went over all the plans again, checking up very carefully on the various details, particularly those discussed with you by telephone.

Meanwhile, you may have received the rough sketches showing the improvements by shifting 18" of length from the south-west end to the north-east end. Kitchen, guest room , and the maids' rooms are all generously proportioned now. There is sufficient space around the guest beds, and kitchen and pantry space is ample for the biggest dinner. All the rooms, including the maids' rooms are of good size, so I don't think Mrs. Frank or you need worry that any room is too small, particularly as the furnishing of the rooms will be carefully laid out.

As to the form of the lower steps of the staircase near the main entrance, we think that the double bend towards the entrance provides a much more inviting shape than when the staircase bends inwards only.

There are, of course, quite a few minor points to be improved upon, after the working drawings are finally made. Therefore, we are expecting your OK for the plans in their present state in order to go ahead with the finishing of the $\frac{1}{4}$" drawings, (plans and elevations), and the preparation of perspectives showing the exterior.

I must confess that I am deeply in love with the whole project and that I expect the house to be very noble in appearance.

With best regards for yourself and Mrs. Frank,

Very sincerely yours,

Walter Gropius

Walter Gropius

WG:L

ABOVE: "I am deeply in love" letter from Walter Gropius.

Family archives, 1939

WALTER GROPIUS AND MARCEL BREUER

ASSOCIATED ARCHITECTS

1430 MASSACHUSETTS AVENUE

CAMBRIDGE, MASS.

TELEPHONE - KIRKLAND 6088

June 12, 1939.

Robert J. Frank, Esq.
1336 Inverness Avenue
Pittsburgh, Pennsylvania.

Dear Mr. Frank:

Regarding our telephone conversation today: I understand that you and Mrs. Frank wish the stair between the first and second floors to have a more transparent effect. I hope to be able to bring you a sketch of the stair this weekend, when, as I understand it, you wish me to come down to Pittsburgh. I will bring with me all the material I have, which will be pretty much completed by then, so that we can discuss everything. Then I can spend the following week completing the material so that it can be estimated.

I will also bring with me a detail for the railing and the outside stair as I would suggest it, and, if I can, another detail, showing the same parts with copper pipes and special copper fittings.

Very sincerely yours,

Marcel Breuer

Marcel Breuer

MB:L

BELOW: Walter Gropius (left), founder of the Bauhaus, and Marcel Breuer (right), one of his leading protégés, brought modernism to the United States in 1937 when Gropius emigrated from Europe to chair the Department of Architecture at Harvard's Graduate School of Design. Robert Frank attended one of his lectures in 1938. In modernism's new approach, he found the inspiration he was seeking for the new family home he wanted to build in Pittsburgh. The Frank House was one of Gropius and Breuer's earliest projects in the U.S. It would ultimately be their largest and most important residential commission, and the only one designed as a total work of art, including structure, furnishings and landscape.

Imagno/Getty Images, 1955 (left); Homer Page, Museum of Modern Art / Licensed by SCALA / Art Resource, NY, 1949 (right)

LEFT: Correspondence between the Franks and the architects often ran to several long letters every week during design and construction. This note from Marcel Breuer discusses their collaboration on the cantilevered stair, a signature feature of the house and, later, of Breuer's design.

Family archive, 1939

July 24, 1939

Mr. Marcel Breuer
1430 Massachusetts Avenue
Cambridge, Massachusetts

Dear Mr. Breuer:

I wired you last night on the subject of a model, as well as various sleeves. I hope this message was clear to you upon receipt.

Mrs. Frank, Alan and myself expect to arrive in Boston early Saturday morning, July 29. I think we can be at your office in Cambridge at 9:00 A.M. or a little before. We would like to see the metal Venetian blinds, as well as pay an official visit to your headquarters. From that point we would like to visit your new home and that of Dr. Gropius.

My mother's car will meet us at the station in Boston, so we will have transportation facilities. It is our hope to get started northward before noon, so these visits will be rather hasty.

Siesel is putting up some battery boards today and the plumber is digging the ditch on our property, so by Wednesday I think we will be able to break the bottle of champagne.

With best wishes.

Very truly yours,

Robert J. Frank

RJF:G

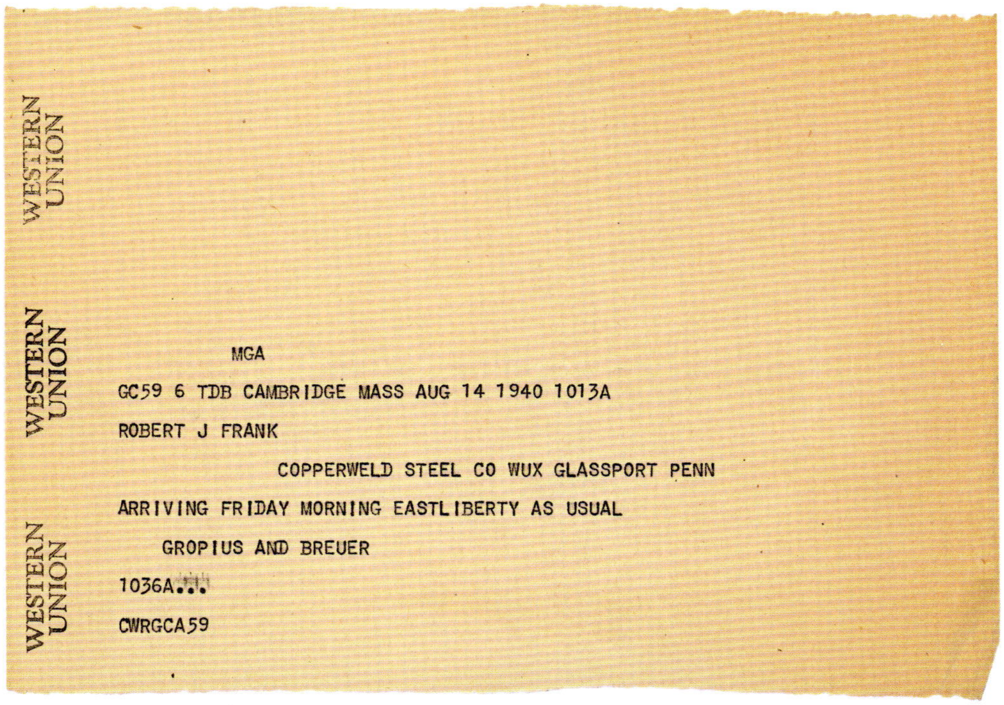

WESTERN UNION

MGA

GC59 6 TDB CAMBRIDGE MASS AUG 14 1940 1013A

ROBERT J FRANK

COPPERWELD STEEL CO WUX GLASSPORT PENN

ARRIVING FRIDAY MORNING EASTLIBERTY AS USUAL

GROPIUS AND BREUER

1036A...

CWRGCA59

LEFT: A telegram describes one of the frequent weekend visits the architects made from Boston to Pittsburgh to select the land, plan the house and oversee the project.

Family archive, 1940

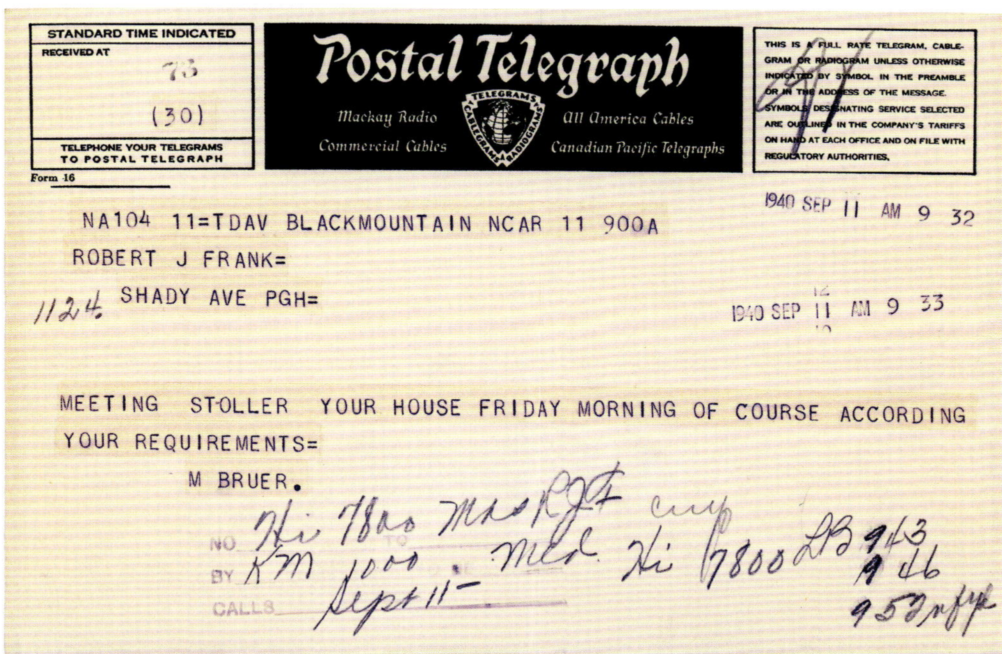

STANDARD TIME INDICATED

RECEIVED AT

(30)

TELEPHONE YOUR TELEGRAMS TO POSTAL TELEGRAPH

Postal Telegraph

Mackay Radio · All America Cables · Commercial Cables · Canadian Pacific Telegraphs

THIS IS A FULL RATE TELEGRAM, CABLEGRAM OR RADIOGRAM UNLESS OTHERWISE INDICATED BY SYMBOL IN THE PREAMBLE OR IN THE ADDRESS OF THE MESSAGE. SYMBOLS DESIGNATING SERVICE SELECTED ARE OUTLINED IN THE COMPANY'S TARIFFS ON HAND AT EACH OFFICE AND ON FILE WITH REGULATORY AUTHORITIES.

Form 16

NA104 11=TDAV BLACKMOUNTAIN NCAR 11 900A 1940 SEP 11 AM 9 32

ROBERT J FRANK=

1124 SHADY AVE PGH= 1940 SEP 11 AM 9 33

MEETING STOLLER YOUR HOUSE FRIDAY MORNING OF COURSE ACCORDING YOUR REQUIREMENTS=

M BRUER.

LEFT: A telegram describes Marcel Breuer's commitment to meet photographer Ezra Stoller on site to oversee the first photography of the finished house, indicating the importance of the project to Breuer and Gropius.

Family archive, 1940

LEFT: A letter from Robert Frank to Marcel Breuer discusses the first meeting between the family and the architects, initiating the project. Cele, Robert and young Alan traveled to Boston, met Gropius and Breuer and toured their recently built homes in Lincoln, Massachusetts.

Family archive, 1939

J. VERNER SCAIFE, JR.

~~XXXXXXXXXXXXX~~
Woodland Road
Pittsburgh, Penna.

March 27, 1939.

Mr. Robert J. Frank,
1336 Inverness Avenue,
Pittsburgh, Pennsylvania.

Dear Mr. Frank:

Will you kindly excuse this much belated acknowledgment of your letter of March 7 which was sent to the attention of Mrs. Clara H. Brown and which later was handed to me on Saturday by Mr. Charles M. Brown.

I purchased Mrs. Clara Brown's property in December, 1937 and, therefore, this explains why the document in regard to the city water main rights was given to me. I sincerely thank you for your courtesy in this matter.

I am glad to know that you have purchased the Kuhn property on Woodland Road and it is my understanding that you will shortly build a new structure on the property. Mrs. Scaife and I had quite a job in fixing up our property but we are delighted with it now and if I can be of any assistance to you in any matters which should come up, please do not hesitate to call upon me.

Looking forward with pleasure to meeting you within the near future, I wish to remain

Yours very truly,

J. Verner Scaife, Jr.

JVS,Jr:L

LEFT: A welcoming letter from across-the-road neighbor J. Verner Scaife, Jr.

Family archive, 1939

ABOVE: Part of the family's collection of glass bottles and jars made in the factory founded by Alan's great-grandfather, William Frank (1819–1891) in Pittsburgh in 1858. The small plant on the banks of the Monongahela River, near a stop on the railroad called Frankstown, was one of the area's first manufacturing companies.

Richard Barnes, 2019

RIGHT: Alan's grandfather, Pittsburgh steel pioneer I W Frank, started as an engineer working for Andrew Carnegie, then went on to build his own business in manufacturing rolling mills and other equipment for steel plants throughout the United States and around the world. In addition to founding his own company, the Frank-Kneeland Machine Company, which became United Engineering & Foundry Company; I W Frank founded or helped establish many of the giants of the steel industry, including Weirton Steel, Great Lakes Steel and National Steel. In 1899, I W Frank was selected by banker J.P. Morgan as the person most qualified to select and negotiate purchase agreements with the steel companies that would become part of the new United States Steel Corporation, the world's largest corporation upon its formation in 1901.

Family archive, 1923

BELOW: A 1900 news article reporting on I W Frank's pivotal role in the formation of United States Steel.

I always thought of the workshop as Dad's workshop. When I looked at the original blueprints a few years ago I was surprised to see he had called it "Alan's Workshop."

Make something useful. Make someone's life a little better. These were the unspoken guideposts when I was young. Sometimes the effort was successful, sometimes not. But the quest was always exciting, and what made life interesting.

When I was growing up, and when my children were growing up, one of our favorite books was *The Little Engine That Could*, a story about a little railroad engine that, when the big powerful engines refused to help, pulled the train over the mountain so the children in the next village could have their toys on Christmas.

My great-grandfather started one of the first manufacturing companies in the Pittsburgh area in the mid-1800s, to make glass bottles and jars that could preserve food over the winter. It was a small plant located near the Frankstown stop of the railroad.

My grandfather, I W Frank, after whom I am named, was one of only a handful of engineers working in Pittsburgh when the steel industry was being built. He first worked for Andrew Carnegie. Then he started his own company to engineer and build the huge rolling mills that made sheet steel to close tolerances at high speeds in the late 1800s and early 1900s, without benefit of electronics or computers. Just superb engineering. The sheet steel was used to make "tin" cans to preserve food and to supply the brand-new automobile industry.

I W Frank founded or helped establish the Frank-Kneeland Machine Company, United Engineering & Foundry Company, Weirton Steel, Great Lakes Steel, National Steel, and United States Steel.

In 1899, J. P. Morgan selected my grandfather as the most qualified person to decide which steel companies should become part of the new United States Steel Corporation that Morgan was forming. I W secured purchase agreements with the companies he thought should be included. At the time of its formation and for many years thereafter, the new United States Steel Corporation was the largest and most important corporation in the world.

A better feeling prevails in the sheet trade. I W Frank of Pittsburg has again been appointed to receive options on the sheet mills, and has a number of them, which will expire on April 1.

The New York Times
Published: January 11, 1900

And yet I never heard from anyone in my family that his or her goal was to make money. It was always a desire to make or do something useful, to make someone's life better.

My grandfather wrote Dad: "All we have is but lent to us, a trust for which we must someday render account."

I know my parents believed that, and I do too. After the stock market collapse in 1929, my grandfather used his own funds to pay off debt of Pittsburgh institutions he believed

were important to the city's future, including the universities, so they could survive the Great Depression.

And in the heroic, inventive era of American architecture, I believe the house is truly another manifestation of that spirit, to make something or do something useful, perhaps better than had been done before.

We spend most of our lives, at home and at work, in the built environment. Who can doubt that growing up, and living in a nurturing space, close to nature, is more likely to produce the kind of men and women that will make the world a better place?

Sharing our home with others, and attempting in some small way to share the understanding of this masterwork of Walter Gropius and Marcel Breuer and my Mother and Dad... was my first job, and as you can see, I am still at it.

Different visitors have had different insights. A visitor from Winterthur, the duPont estate in Delaware, called the house the absolute height of elegance in twentieth-century architecture. He pointed out the elaborate natural and subtle color harmony of each individual room ensemble, and that each room's color palette is a variation on a theme that threads through the house and together is beautifully balanced.

Toshiko Mori, former head of the Harvard Graduate School of Design, observed, "It is so sensuous."

My good friend, classmate, and fellow editor of the *Harvard Crimson*, Frank Cahouet, who moved to Pittsburgh in the late 1980s to serve as CEO of Mellon Bank, visited the house, and remarked on the extraordinary courage my parents had to invest a million dollars during the Great Depression to create this work of art.

And in the early 1990s another friend of mine called to say that J Carter Brown, former director of the National Gallery of Art in Washington, had looked at my house many times from the road and would very much appreciate an invitation to come over. A few weeks later, on a beautiful fall afternoon, he arrived.

I remember after I showed him the house, he sat down on the stone window sill in the dining room and looked at the sculptured travertine and English sycamore walls, the magnificent pearwood dining table whose transparent legs were illuminated by the sun, and the graceful pearwood chairs covered in soft chocolate-colored cotton. Carter sat and did not speak for a long time. He looked as though he were in heaven. Finally, he said quietly, "This is the nation's crown jewel."

I agree, and suggest that the house is more than an architectural masterwork—even more than Carter Brown's "crown jewel." It is a rare thing—a unique and beautiful family home, a work of art whose creation was the result of the rarest and most precious of motivations. Love—the love of my parents for each other and for their children.

Alan and his granddaughter Suzanne. Four generations of the family have made the Frank House their home.

Kimberly Frank Shaw, 2007

A CELEBRATION OF LIVING
BY KENNETH FRAMPTON

The Alan I W Frank House is by far the largest and the most luxurious of the homes designed by émigré Bauhaus architects Walter Gropius and Marcel Breuer during their North American partnership as well as throughout their individual practices. They had collaborated in various ways before, not only during the time that Gropius was the director of the Bauhaus but also soon after their immigration to the United States. The commission for this house came about after the client, the industrialist Robert J. Frank, heard Gropius lecture in 1938 on the theme of the new architecture and the Bauhaus, a topic that had been the subject of a book by Gropius. While both architects contributed equally to the initial parti of the house, it is evident from the detailing and the highly expressive use of materials that Breuer profoundly influenced its furnishings, particularly the bespoke furniture that he designed expressly for each space, pieces that were never put into general production and are unique within the spectrum of his general output.

Upon approaching the house, which is situated on a verdant site with mature trees in the prestige neighborhood of Pittsburgh's Shadyside, one becomes immediately aware of its facing, large panels of three-inch-thick Kasota stone that involved the use of a crane to manipulate and lay the heavy slabs into their appointed positions. One is equally struck by the refined way in which this revetment is tooled over its entire surface. Breuer's sensibility is evident in the random stone paving of the entry, which is fully enclosed on both sides by glass blocks and recalls the generous foyer of Breuer's Doldertal Apartments, built in Zurich in 1936, particularly the paving on the floor and the exotic indoor planting—an ambience augmented by an elliptical side seat, covered in calfskin, and a small glass table. The honorific status of this foyer is represented externally by inclined frosted glass panels poised on either side of the front door plus adjacent freestanding steel columns supporting the concrete roof, the whole having a highly sculptural, quasi-classical character. This luminous assembly announcing the entrance is the sculptural counter-form of the reinforced concrete and steel stair linking the large open first-floor terrace that runs through the house to the greensward immediately in front of the indoor swimming pool.

The three-story orthogonal form of the building is modulated by the regular spacing of the steel frame and by the horizontal fenestration, which is maintained throughout save for the bow window of the main stair, which protrudes slightly beyond the front of the house for its entire height. In addition to the Kasota stone, a randomly laid fieldstone wall was built beneath the staircase window. This incidental use of local fieldstone had already become a stylistic trope of the Gropius and Breuer practice, as is evident in the small houses that they built for their own occupation in Lincoln, Massachusetts, at around the same time. The occasional use of glass-block walling is the other familiar Breuer-esque feature to be found throughout the Frank House, where it occurs not only at the entry but also at the rear of the house in the form of a freestanding wall, screening the servants' terrace from the garden. This material appears again in a skylight illuminating the depth of the indoor pool, which is lit at the other end of the volume by two large steel-framed sliding glass doors. When these doors are open the space evokes the feeling of swimming at a level above the site due to

RIGHT: Breuer's sensibility is evident in the random stone paving of the entry, which is fully enclosed by glass.

Ezra Stoller, 1940

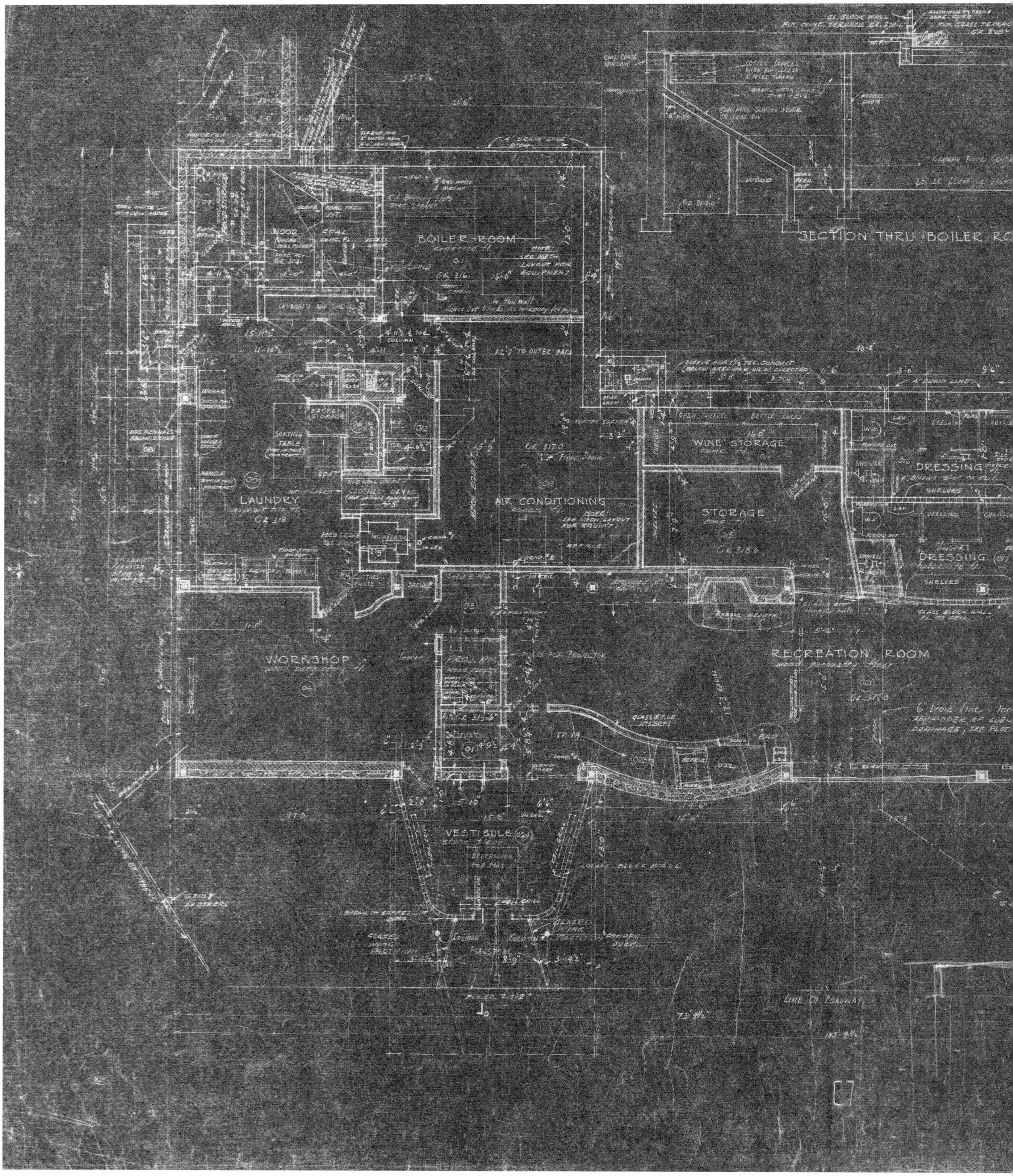
BOILER ROOM
LAUNDRY
AIR CONDITIONING
WINE STORAGE
STORAGE
DRESSING
DRESSING
WORKSHOP
RECREATION ROOM
VESTIBULE
GLASS BLOCK WALL

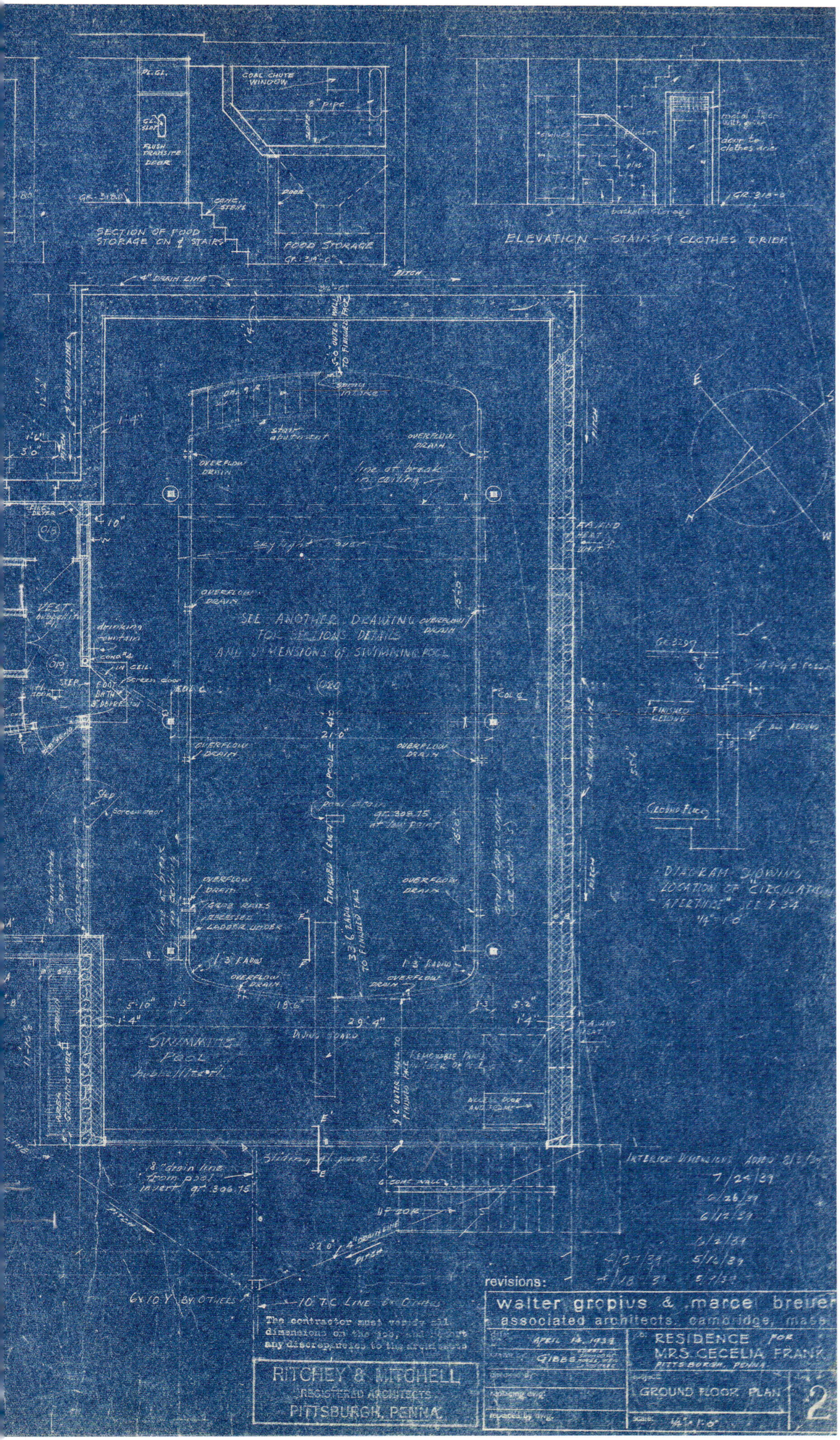

LEFT: One of 254 blueprints made for the Frank House. It details the ground floor which, in addition to the pool and recreation room, includes the workshop, the wine cellar, storage room, and the laundry, as well as the boiler room and air conditioning room.

Family archive, 1939

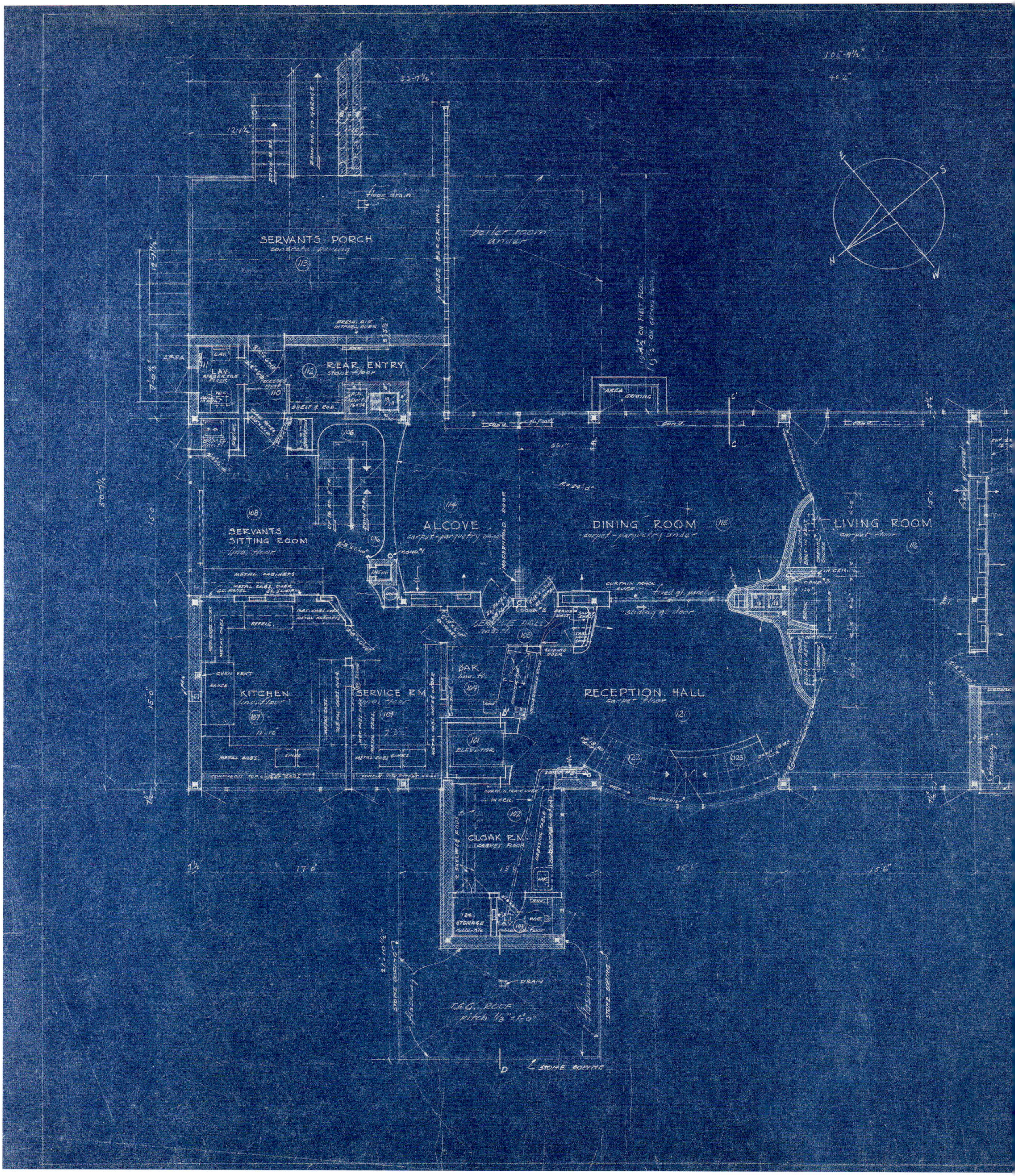

SERVANTS PORCH
boiler room under
REAR ENTRY
SERVANTS SITTING ROOM
ALCOVE
DINING ROOM
LIVING ROOM
KITCHEN
SERVICE RM
BAR
ELEVATOR
RECEPTION HALL
CLOAK RM
T.&G. ROOF
STONE COPING

LEFT: The first floor blueprint reveals an innovative design that encourages connection and flow from room to room.

Family archive, 1939

Jay Turnbull, Principal, Page & Turnbull; Alan, and an engineer from Wiss, Janney, Elstener Associates, review preservation plans.

Family archives, 2012

Three stonemasons and Alan place a new 800-pound Kasota capstone atop the chimney. The lightning rod is one of many Copperweld lightning rods that protect the house.

Family archives, 2012

the fall of the land toward the road. A number of utilitarian elements are also found on this floor, including a workshop, a wine cellar, storage, and the laundry room, as well as a boiler room and a relatively large volume given over to the air conditioning. The servants' stair also starts at this level and continues throughout the building to the top of the house.

The first floor is effectively the piano nobili of the house although, due to the slope of the site, this main reception level, one floor above grade at the front of the house, is at the level of the garden in the rear. As is invariably the case with Breuer's houses, this principal level is divided by a freestanding fireplace and chimneybreast, which in this instance, assumes an unusual aerodynamic form, faced throughout in polished travertine. This treatment gives each of the three internal spaces—the reception hall, the dining room, and the living room—an honorific aura, so that each is accorded a setting appropriate to the reception of large social gatherings. In this way, aside from serving as a family home, the house was designed to accommodate sociocultural receptions, largely organized by the client's wife, Cecelia Frank. Well before the house was built, Cecelia had already established her position in Pittsburgh as a local patron of the arts, most particularly of music and the theater, which surely accounts not only for the travertine but also for the amenities provided on the first floor: namely a cloakroom, built out over the entry and a bar, which, faced in a veneer of English pearwood, creates a welcoming atmosphere to offset the formality of the stone. This was the appointed space for an aperitif before proceeding to the dining room via a double glass door. The dining room could easily accommodate twenty-four persons at a single sitting, with the table capable of being added to in sections according to the size of the party. Normally this dining room was carpeted but this could be readily removed to reveal an oak floor beneath; a more appropriate surface for dancing.

The evening's entertainment ritual was usually completed by retiring to the living room, where the company could assemble about the travertine central fireplace, sitting within the curved form of a custom-made, well-upholstered six-seater couch or on the inglenook seats on either side of the hearth and additional easy chairs nearby. The appointment of these three rooms recalls the mores of the previous century in that the living room has been given a certain feminine inflection as opposed to the masculine aura of the adjacent study to which access is more restricted. The conservatory at one end of the study serves as a mediatory element since it is equally visible from both the living and dining spaces. This spatial sequence also makes use of a folding screen that slides on a track so that the children's breakfast room can be temporarily separated from the dining room.

All the furniture throughout the house was designed by the architects including the dining chairs by Breuer, which, apart from the upholstery, were constructed of cutout and bent plywood sheets faced in a veneer of pearwood. These figurative elements become even more animate in the case of the house's easy chairs and a *chaise longue* that Breuer designed in various forms and fabrics. All this work is quite removed from the functionalist chromium-plated tubular steel pieces that Breuer designed and produced in the second half of the 1920s. The bespoke chairs, fabricated out of laminated sheets of exotic wood, included a more elaborately articulated and convenient version of the Isokon *chaise longue* that Breuer had designed for Jack Pritchard in London, prior to leaving for the United States in 1937. Unlike his previous

All the furniture in the house was designed by the architects, including this pearwood and Lucite table.

Sotheby's, 2005

The chairs, designed by Breuer, were constructed of cutout plywood sheets faced in a veneer of pearwood.

Sotheby's, 2005

Marcel Breuer graphite drawings
and chairs for the house.

Marcel Breuer Digital Archives

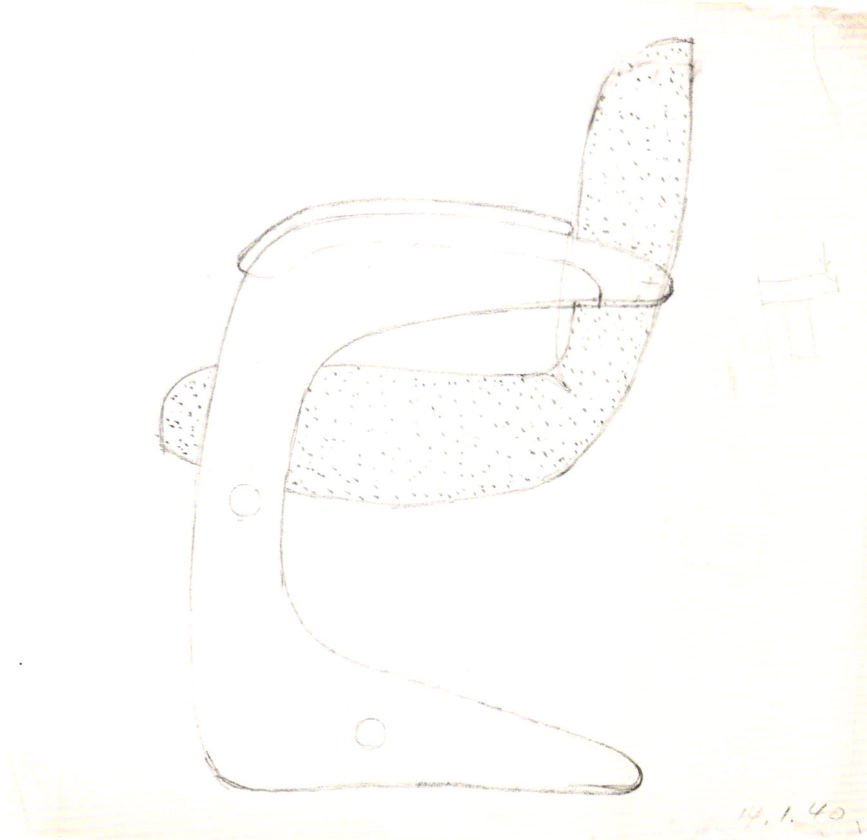

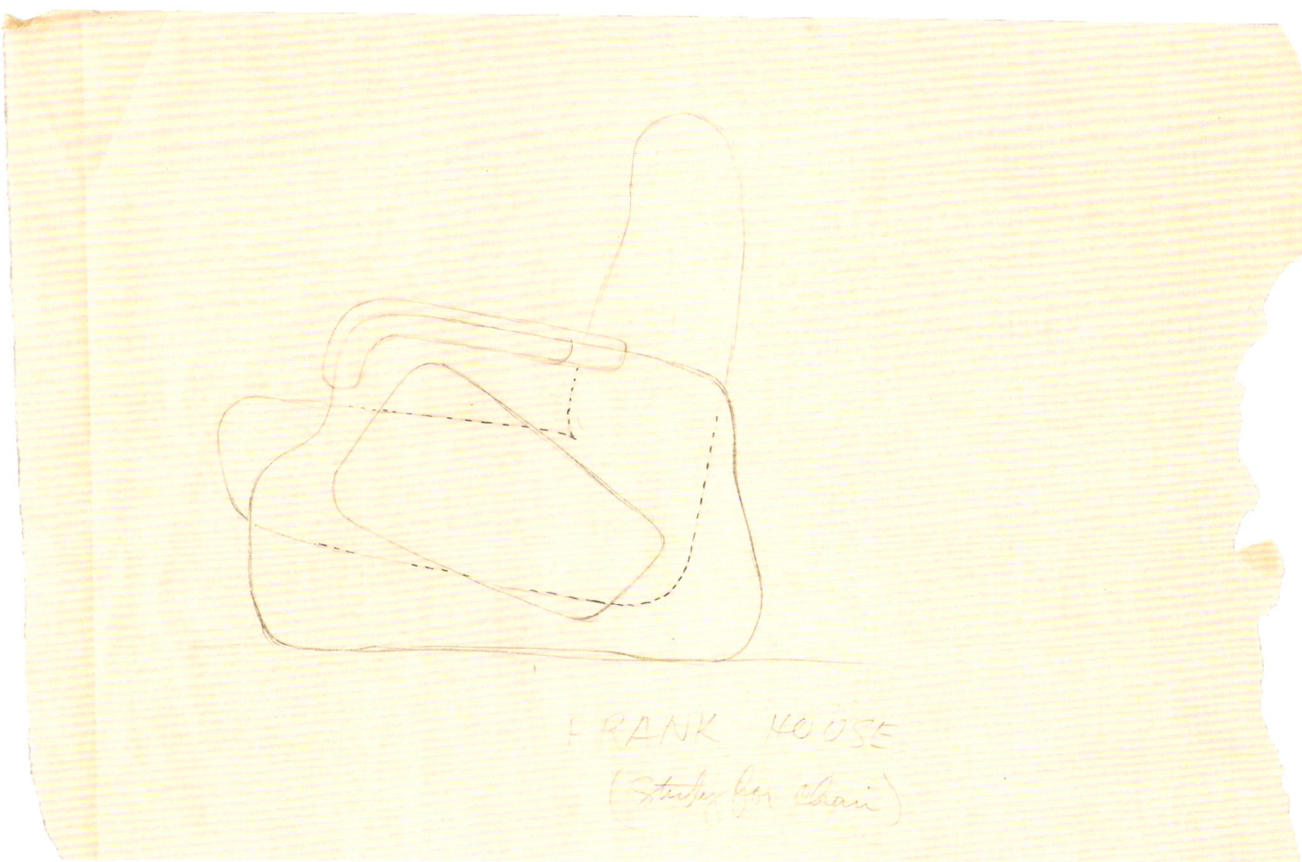

Ezra Stoller, 1940

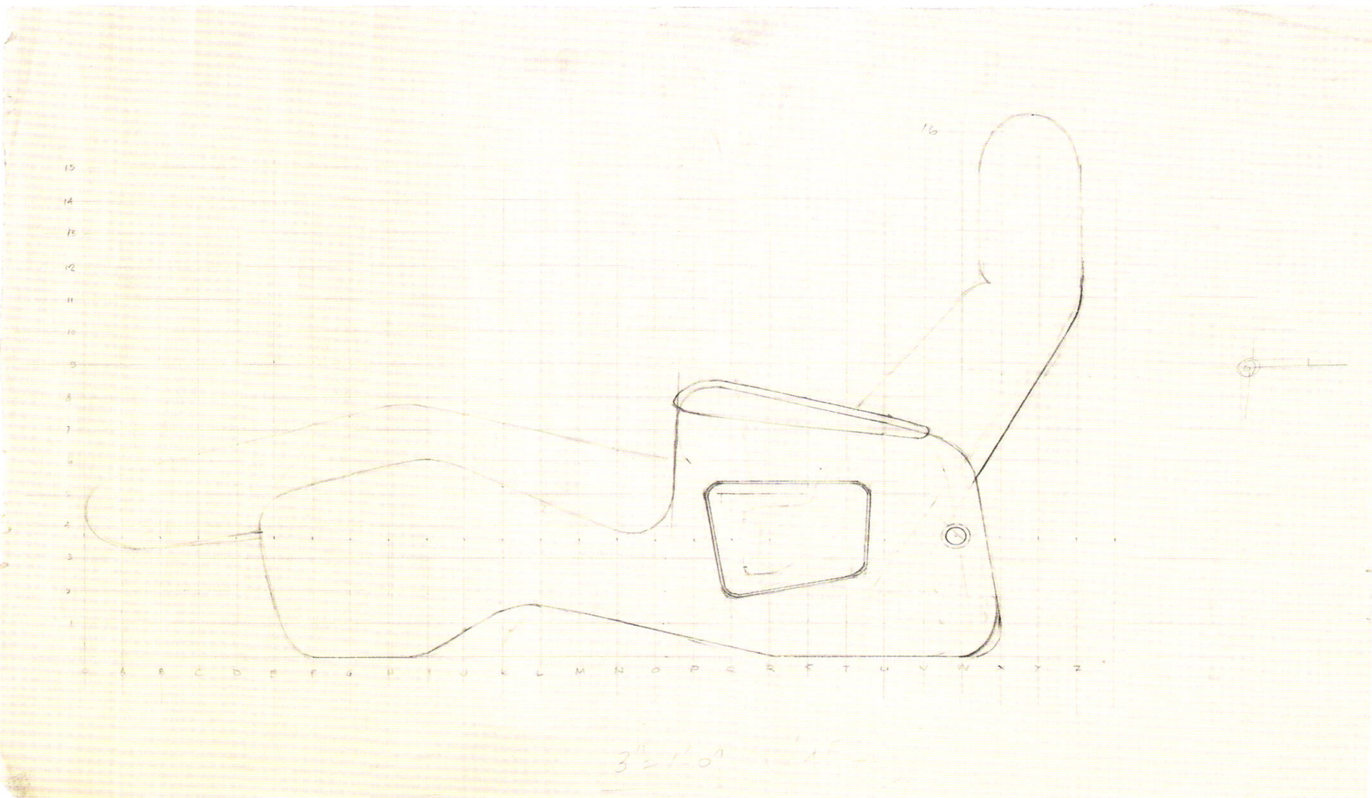

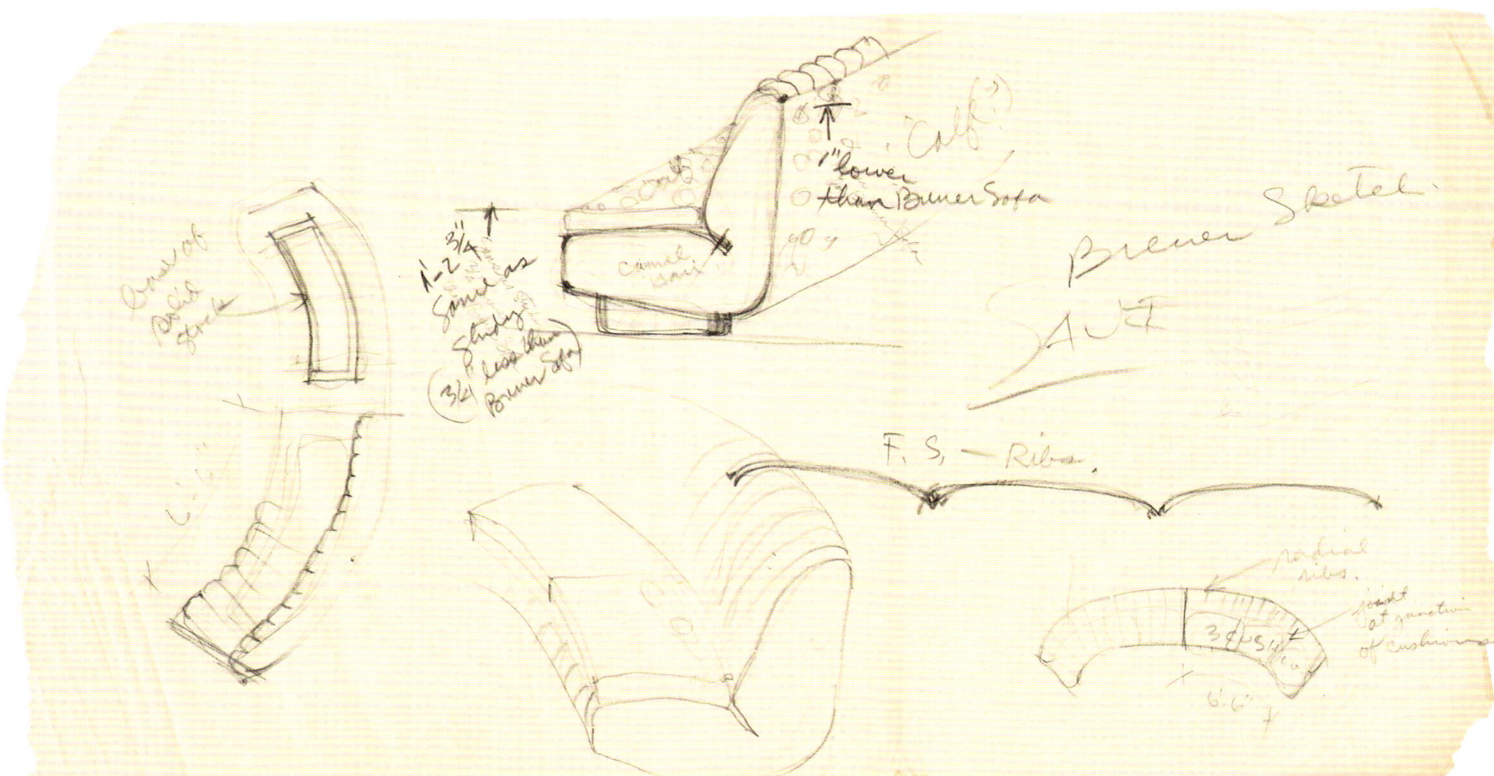

Drawings for a bespoke sofa and chaise longue chairs, fabricated out of laminated sheets of exotic wood, include a more elaborately articulated version of the Isokon chaise longue that Breuer had designed in London prior to leaving for the United States in 1937.

Marcel Breuer Digital Archives

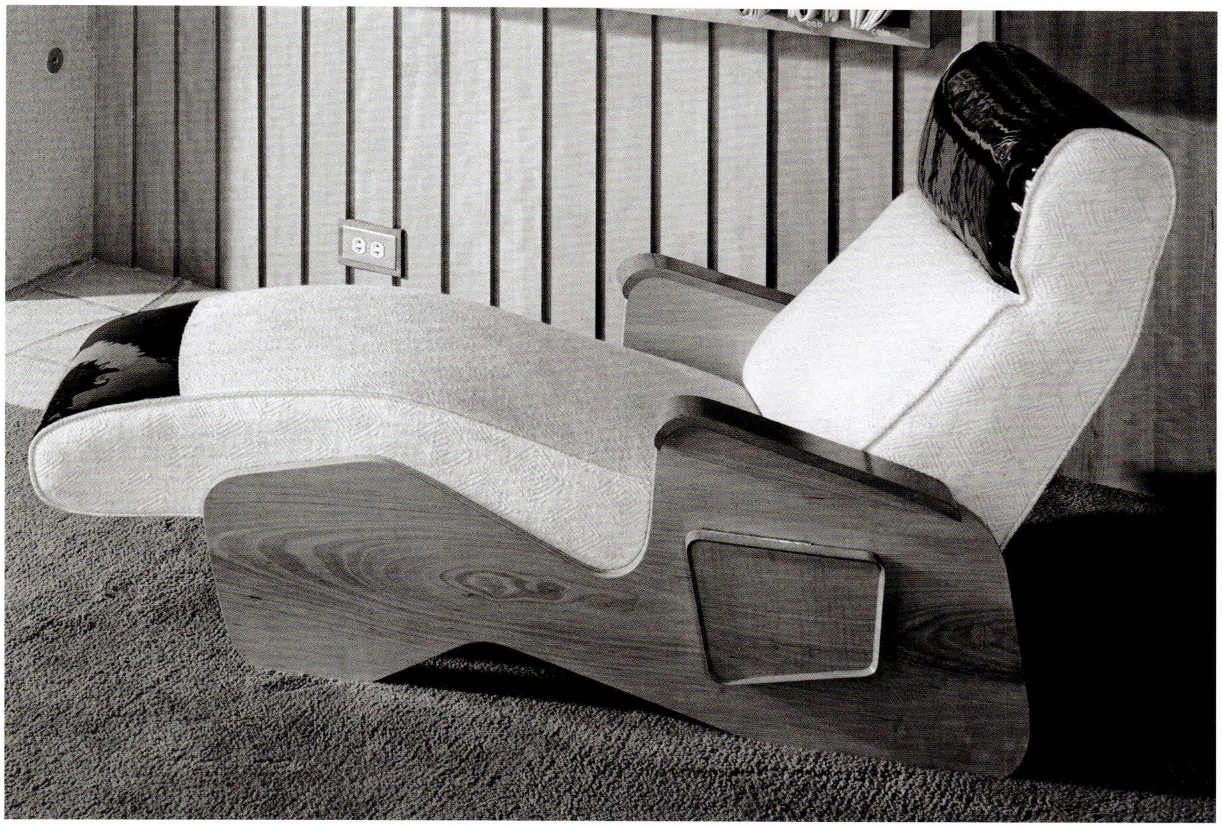

Ezra Stoller, 1940

furniture, these exotic pieces seem to have been influenced by the organic sculptures of Jean Arp and may also be seen, in retrospect, as being close to the design work of his fellow Hungarian and former Bauhaus colleague, László Moholy-Nagy, who at this time was establishing his Institute of Design in Chicago.

Breuer's furniture, designed exclusively for the Frank House, contributes to the undeniably theatrical sensibility that pervades the house at different moments in what is otherwise an unequivocally modern work. This ethos is evident in the curved form of the principal stair, built entirely of reinforced concrete with cantilevered treads that gain their support from the bent beam of the concrete balustrade. These treads stop short of the bow window housing the stair, creating the illusion that the stair is miraculously suspended in space. This dematerialized image is further enhanced by a tubular handrail bracketed off the metal fenestration of the window.

This total work of art experimented with the latest materials of the day, including Lucite table legs and door handles, the latter possessing a luminosity that rendered them visible in the dark. The client was all in favor of using the latest electrical devices, such as an inter-floor communication system and the latest means for electrostatic filtration and dehumidification of the conditioned air. Otherwise the house was warmed by central heating via concealed radiators. The house was also the occasion for discreet, almost unnoticeable technical innovations by Robert Frank such as a pneumatic system that, when a damper built into the flue of each fireplace was opened, had the effect of closing the return air ducts and shutting off the flow of hot water to the radiators in that room.

On occasion the architects employed special finishes such as cork tiles for the floors and the walls in the male bathrooms and large panels of glass in cream or light blue on the walls, with matching baths, in the bathrooms designed for the two daughters. In the main bathroom-dressing space, opening off the master bedroom and used exclusively by the client's wife, is a light wood veneer of English sycamore applied to a built-in dressing table and desk. These furnishings are accompanied by burgundy glass panels lining the walls of the combined bath and shower. The house makes extensive use of curtains, often vertically as transitional elements and at other times as diaphanous linings softening the presence of the venetian blinds, which provide sun screening for the horizontal fenestration deployed throughout the house.

The full complement of rooms on the second floor includes, besides the principal bedrooms and their respective bathrooms, a guest room and a servants' room. This level, served by the elevator and by the last flight of the main stair, is focused about an intimate family room with a central granite fireplace and hearth, as is the recreation space on the ground floor anchored by a central fieldstone fireplace.

Apart from a storage room and sleeping accommodation for three servants, the roof level, accessed only by the service stair and the elevator, is largely occupied by a timber deck that makes up almost half of the roof surface. This deck includes open-air showers to be used after rooftop sunbathing. In addition, a reinforced timber floor area inserted within the deck provides a suitable surface for dancing.

A total work of art, the Frank House experimented with the latest materials, including Lucite table legs and door handles. The latter possessed a luminosity that rendered them visible in the dark.

Richard Barnes, 2019

As the Ezra Stoller photographs taken at the completion of the house suggest, there was something intrinsically theatrical and inherently festive about the fully furnished house, amounting to a richly elaborated dwelling that was not only designed to serve the well-being of the family but also to provide a fitting environment within which to host and celebrate the dramatic and musical arts of the city, as well as receive prestigious public figures who were playing or on the verge of playing key roles in the development of the culture and society of Pittsburgh. At the time of its completion, just prior to Pearl Harbor and the outbreak of the World War II, this was an ideal house for a soiree as opposed to the heavy, somewhat conservative character of large bourgeois mansions in various historical styles that, then as now, surrounded it on every side. At the same time, the recreation room, the swimming pool, and dancing space on the roof would suggest, it was also something of a weekend house. In this respect it may be appropriately compared to Alvar Aalto's Villa Mairea at Noormarkku, in Finland, of virtually the same date—also a family house for an industrialist that had an equally hedonistic program, projected for a larger and more bucolic site. Like the Villa Mairea, the Frank House is a swansong to the optimism of the 1930s and, in this regard, it is fitting that it was designed by two refugee architects who left Germany soon after 1933. However, by the late 1930s, neither Gropius nor Breuer were young men, and for them as for their clients, the Frank House represented a new beginning—a golden moment that, due to the encroaching shadow of war, would prove to be unrepeatable.

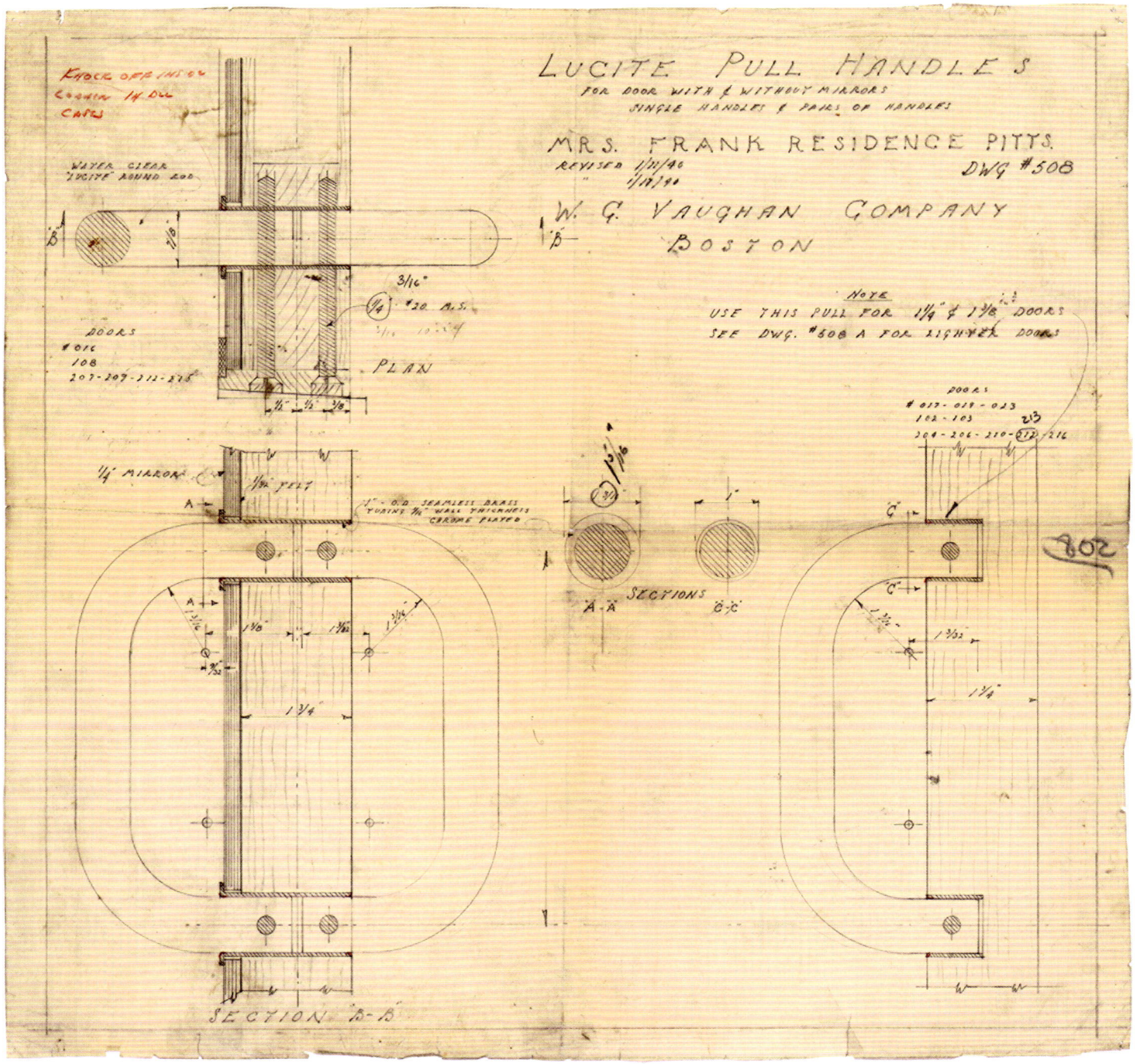

Lucite door handle specifications from hardware manufacturer W C Vaughn of Boston, Massachusetts.

W C Vaughn Co., 1940

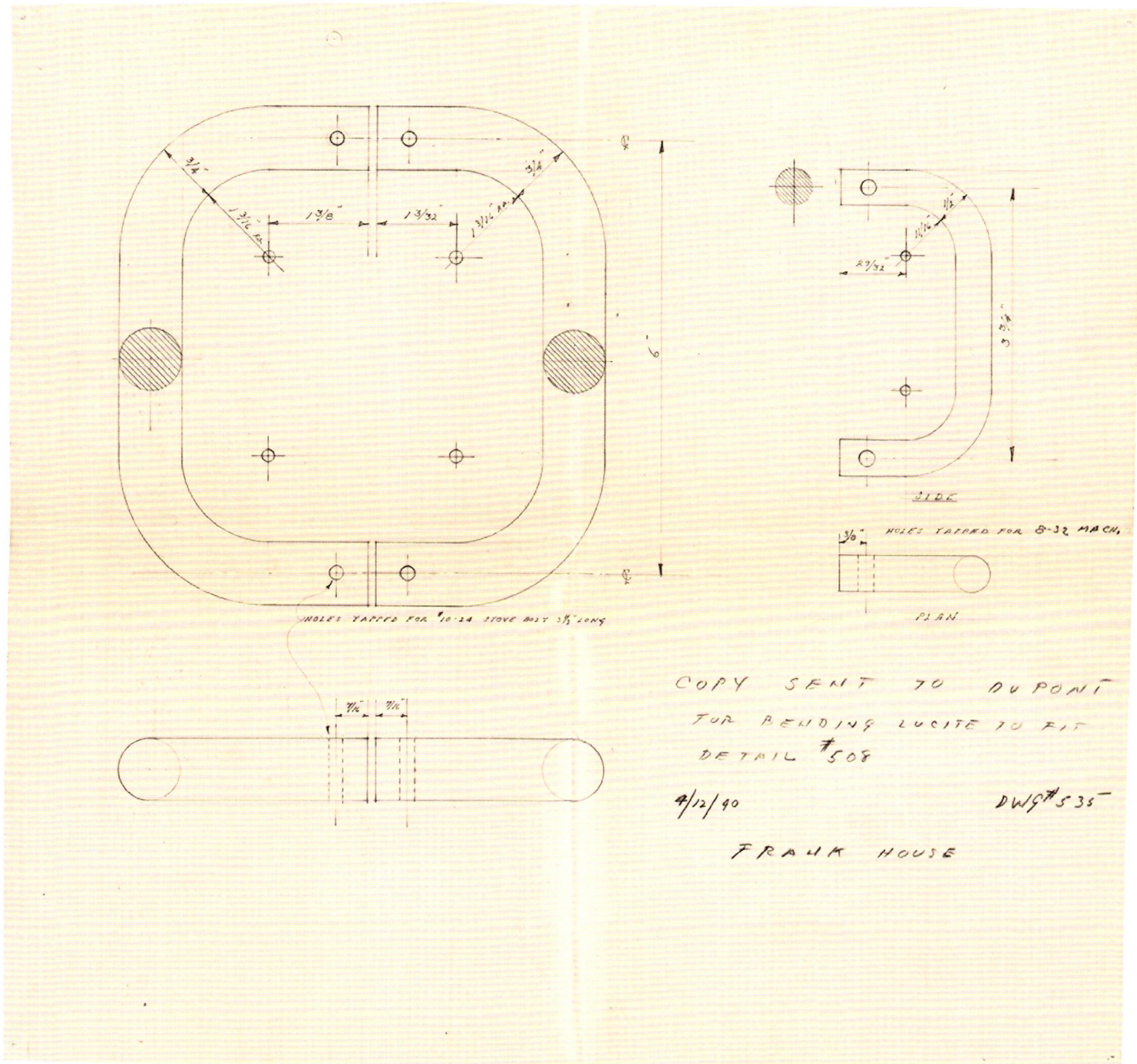

Specifications sent to DuPont for fabricating the Lucite handles.

W C Vaughn Co., 1940

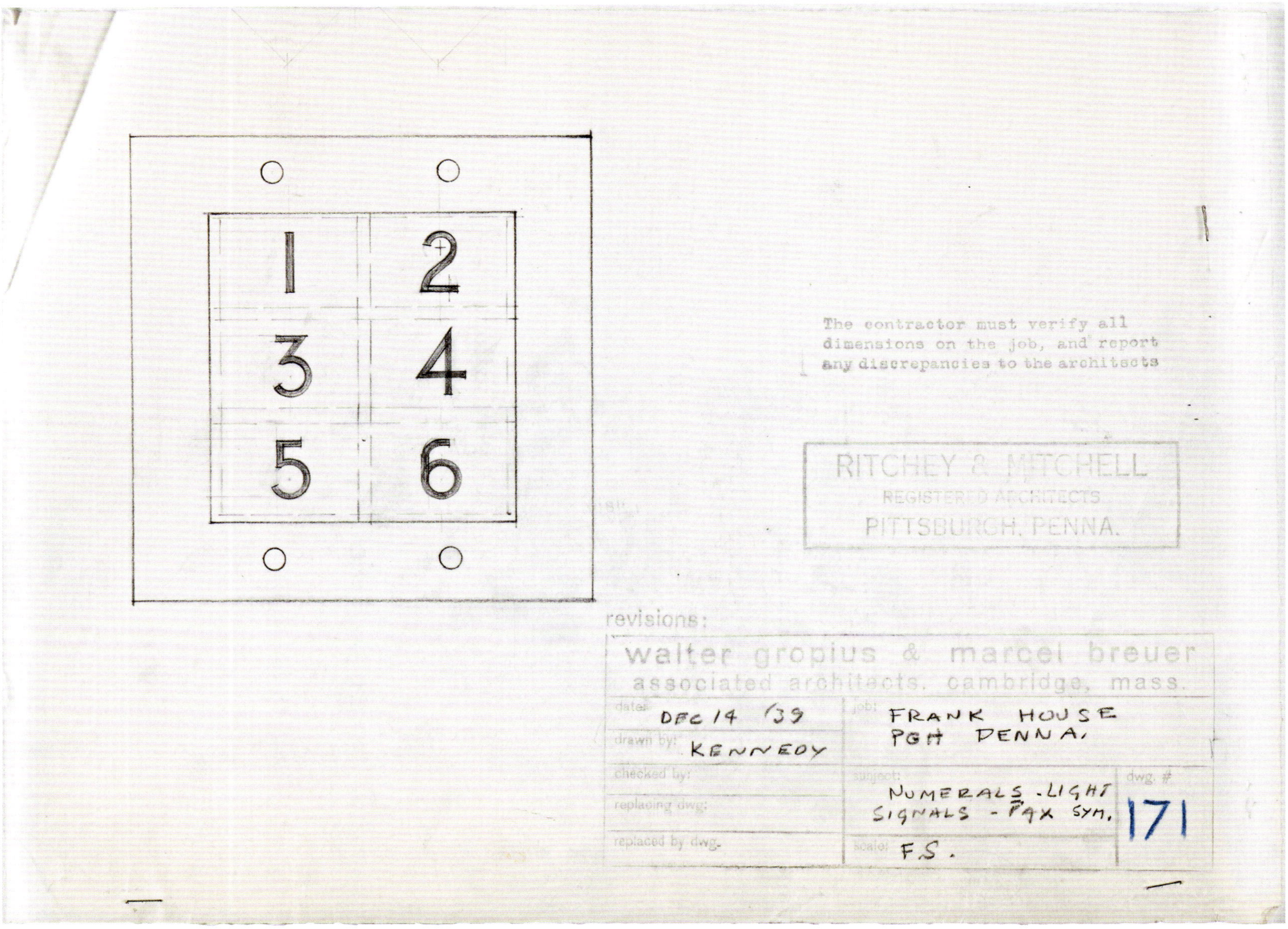

Plans for a light signal system invented by Cele Frank that indicates incoming telephone calls and other information.

Harvard Art Museums, 1940

The light signal.

Alan I W Frank, 2019

Gropius and Breuer designed lighting fixtures to illuminate a room with a warm glow by directing light onto the ceiling and walls.

Richard Pare, 2007

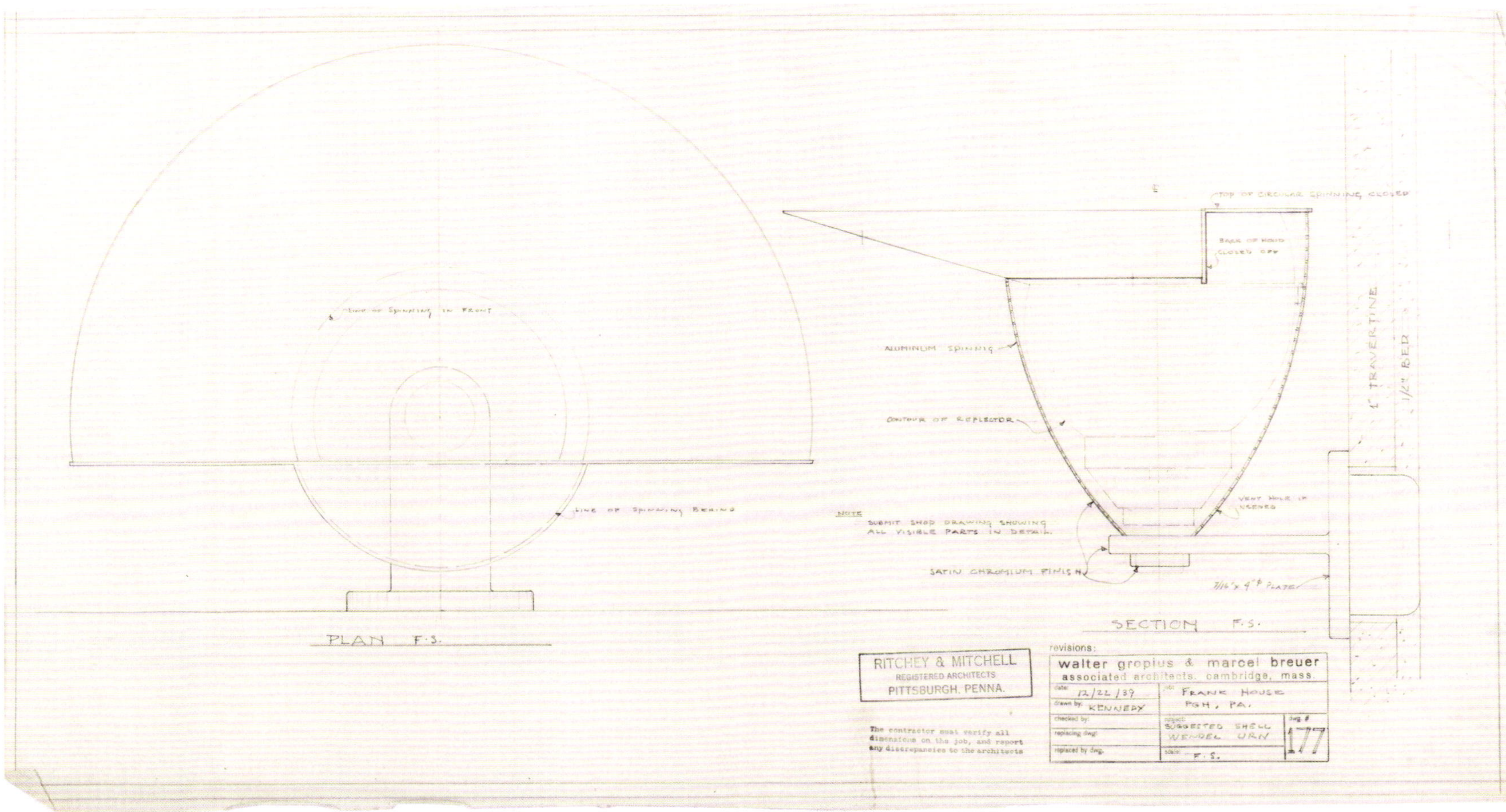

Drawing for lighting fixture.

Harvard Art Museums, 1940

NEW WAYS IN THE NEW WORLD BY BARRY BERGDOLL

This essay was originally published in HÄUSER Magazine *1/2009, Hamburg, Germany, in commemoration of the ninetieth anniversary of the Bauhaus.*

In Robert J. and Cecelia Frank, Pittsburgh engineer/industrialist and his wife, Walter Gropius and Marcel Breuer found a rare client, willing and capable of providing them latitude to realise the Bauhaus dream of a comprehensive environment in their newly adopted homeland. The 1938 commission included landscape and buildings—house and free-standing 4-car garage—and a programme of specially designed furniture, fabrics and lighting fixtures.

Not since Berlin industrialist Adolf Sommerfeld commissioned Gropius had the designer enjoyed a chance to work with a client to realise a house as a total work of art and a laboratory for technological innovations. While the Sommerfeld House, destroyed in World War II, is featured in every history of modernism, the Frank House stands virtually unchanged, but largely undiscovered, seventy years after it was designed. As innovative and as unusual in the Gropius and Breuer oeuvre as the Sommerfeld House, and likewise the result of an intense give-and-take with an engaged client, it is one of the best-kept secrets of American modernism.

Lovingly preserved by the couple's youngest child, Alan I W Frank, who was a young boy when his parents worked with the two ex-Bauhaus masters to create a home that could be one of Pittsburgh's best social gatherings as well as private quarters for each of the five members of the family, it is poised to be transformed into a museum.

Richard Barnes's new colour photographs capture the colours and textures, spatial effects and atmosphere, that make the house a threshold in the transformation of the Bauhaus aesthetic in America. Unlike the Meisterhäuser at Dessau, where a machined aesthetic of stucco rendered walls and floating boxes defined a rigorous geometric approach to composition, the Frank House achieves effects through gently swelling curves set in facades of long horizontal lines, exterior walls of warmly honey-coloured Kasota stone (from Minnesota) clad over a steel skeleton, all set upon a rugged base of local field stone, echoed in the garden's terrace walls. Throughout the client's repeated request in letters for "a warm and friendly feeling" is echoed in the architect's exploration of a new architectural palette.

The great three-storey window which swells in the facade behind the circular stair sweeps visitors from the ground-floor entry and recreational area to the first-floor living floor—at grade with the back garden—and then rises to a family bedroom level. It is derived from the combination of curtain wall glazing in front of the Bauhaus stair; but here the stair is sensuously curved and cantilevered. The theme is echoed in a sculptural exterior stair of concrete taking visitors from the front to the back garden via an open terrace.

Effects are achieved through natural materials set in contrast with industrial products—fieldstone and glass brick—through contrasts of light and heavy, and through dramatic lighting and staging of movement on the wooded, sloping site. The spatial experiments with applied primary colours of the 1920s give way to a composition of natural materials, brilliantly nestled into the slope of the hillside. This shift was paralleled in works of Le Corbusier (Maison de Weekend near Paris), Mies van der Rohe (Resor House project in Wyoming), and Alvar Aalto (Villa Mairea, Noormarkku, Finland) as well as that other great Pittsburgh masterpiece of the 1930s, Frank Lloyd Wright's Fallingwater, with its revolutionary combination of concrete and natural fieldstone. The Frank House must be added to this list of 1930s masterpieces in which the modern was realigned with the natural and the organic.

In 1938 Robert Frank had heard Gropius—newly appointed to head the architecture school at Harvard—lecture, and met Breuer. Frank entrusted these émigré modernists with realizing his dream of a large house for a family of three children and a future life of entertaining, a bold gesture in socially and architecturally conservative Pittsburgh. By May 1939 two adjacent sites had been acquired and cleared; work was underway on the sweeping driveway through the site which stages the house and sets up the dramatic path that continues in the stair which, in turn, organizes movement through the main interiors, a complex programme of spaces, flawlessly orchestrated around a few major themes: the sweeping stair, the wish-bone shaped free-standing chimney core clad in travertine, and strip windows opening the long and relatively shallow house to the leafy front lawn and terraced back garden.

Breuer was given responsibility for the full programme of furnishing the house. Various furniture designs and fixtures were developed, using new resins and manufacturing techniques and incorporating Lucite, a recently developed type of acrylic glass. If in the 1920s Breuer had floated furniture by making cantilevered frames of tubular steel, now he experimented with floating an entire table above transparent table legs. No less innovative were experiments with built-in lighting, even a design for bedside lights that would target reading material without illuminating the room. Frank's correspondence with Gropius and Breuer runs to hundreds of pages; during the construction, suggestions and queries filled 7 to 10-page letters, often several such a week. The house became a "machine for living" as Gropius had called for at the Bauhaus: it incorporated an integral system for cleaning air (necessary in smog-bound industrial Pittsburgh of the period), an internal phone system, built-in projection equipment to turn the recreation room into a cinema, and an experimental technique of relating the water for the indoor swimming pool to the heating and cooling systems of the house.

As the design was nearing its final form Gropius paused in a letter to Robert J. Frank: "I must confess that I am deeply in love with the whole project and that I expect the house to be very noble in appearance." In its myriad innovations it was at once unique in Breuer and Gropius's career, and the seedbed of much to come.

THE LAND: ESSENTIAL CONTEXT FOR THE BIRTH OF MODERNISM IN PITTSBURGH
BY CHARLES A BIRNBAUM

> *Gardens, like houses, are built of space. Gardens are fragments of space set aside by the planes of terraces and walls and disciplined foliage. Until now we have defined too nicely the differences between that space which is roofed and within the house and that which is left outside and around the house. We did not see, until the architect threw down his walls, that the space of house and that of garden are parts of a single organism; that the secret of unity lies in a unity of spatial sequences. . . . The garden flows into and over the house. . . . The house reaches out into the garden with walls and terraced enclosures that continue its rhythms and share its grace. The concordant factor is the new quality given to space..*
>
> —Joseph Hudnut, first dean of Harvard University's Graduate School of Design[1]

When Joseph Hudnut, the first dean of Harvard University's Graduate School of Design (GSD), penned the essay "The Modern Garden" for GSD professor and author Christopher Tunnard's second edition of *Gardens in the Modern Landscape* in 1948 (the widely influential treatise was first published a decade earlier), he could well have had in mind the Cecelia and Robert Frank House[2] nestled in Pittsburgh's leafy and picturesque Shadyside neighborhood, with its terraced site offering borrowed views to the then-booming downtown area. Built from 1939 to 1940, with the landscape completed soon thereafter, the Frank property is among the most significant modernist residential designs by well-known master architects.

This historically significant commission was constructed during the foremost era of the emergence of modernism in American architecture—and the birth of modernist landscape architecture.

STEPPING BACK

It is both exciting and worthwhile to reconsider the historic designed landscape of the Frank property within the context of the prevailing attitudes toward modernism espoused at the GSD, ushered in with the arrival of Bauhaus founder Walter Gropius in 1937. In fact, the Frank House today still powerfully illustrates the convergence, and some might even say collision, of American and European identities that was then playing out at the GSD.

LEFT: Wisteria blossoms hang from a stone sculpture by Marcel Breuer, placed outside the dining room.

Alan I W Frank, 2010

Author Anthony Alofsin noted that, during this explosive period, "radical European modernist attitudes overwhelmed a nascent American modernism peeking out from progressive efforts at reform. This collision took place at the GSD from the late 1930s through the 1940s, when the school became the center of modern design education in America."[3] And, unsurprisingly, at the center of this movement was Gropius. In fact, all of the key players at the Frank House and, by extension, those who would later serve as ambassadors for modernism in Pittsburgh for decades to come, can be traced to the GSD and its cauldron of ideas then brimming with excitement.

As evidenced by the title blocks on the project drawings, Walter Gropius and Marcel Breuer, who taught at Harvard from 1937 to 1946, were the "Associated Architects," joined by Pittsburgher Dahlen "Dahl" Ritchey, of Ritchey & Mitchell, listed as "Registered Architects." Ritchey, who was among the earliest alums to study under Gropius at the GSD and graduated first in his class, supervised the project's construction. It is worth noting that John O. Simonds, although not part of the project's team, graduated from the GSD in 1938. With Harvard's GSD as the incubator and exporter, and the Frank House providing an opportunity for a pioneering foray into modernism, the local ambassadors were empowered to both proselytize and lead by design.

THE HARVARD REVOLUTION AND LANDSCAPE ARCHITECTURE

Three of John Simonds's classmates at the GSD, Garrett Eckbo, James C. Rose, and Dan Kiley, were influenced by Gropius and Breuer to great effect. This trio, whom Simonds held in high regard, led the "Harvard Revolution," a student revolt against the traditional Beaux-Arts style. The three published a series of articles in *Pencil Points* (now *Progressive Architecture*) from 1938 to 1939, including Rose's essay, "Articulate Form in Landscape Design" in February 1939. Here at the Frank House, one can almost sense the design team's response to Rose's plea: "Wherever man goes, we find a reorganization of nature. The fact is the sole justification for the profession of landscape design, and our job is to provide a more skillful arrangement for greater utility and for the expression of contemporary living."[4]

Within the context of the ideas taking root at Harvard, one can see how this revolutionary Pittsburgh commission took inspiration from modern art to complement the natural forms the site offered. The result was a landscape conceived to introduce new shapes, materials, and spatial relationships. Moreover, the modernist principles on display in the Frank House landscape would appear in other projects by Ritchey and Simonds for decades to come, including Mellon Square (1955, John and Phil Simonds and architects Mitchell & Ritchey), Equitable Life Insurance Plaza (1955, Simonds and Simonds), and Allegheny Commons (1966, Simonds and Simonds).

THE FRANK HOUSE LANDSCAPE

A review of the 1939 Plot Plan of the trapezoidal-shaped parcel shows a property that still possesses a high degree of design integrity. The historic core of the approximately two-acre site fronts on East Woodland Road. It is topographically dramatic with a fifty-two-foot grade differential from the front (north) upward to the rear (south).

The layout of the property fits within the historic narrative and design continuum of the Shadyside community. The parcel's frontage includes a picturesque approach-road dotted with large-canopy shade trees, with a ravine on the east side and a meandering naturalistic stone walk on the west. The retention of large shade trees, some centuries old, in this residential setting provides mystery and continuity for the nineteen-thousand-square-foot house, not to mention privacy.

But the major innovation comes at the rear of the property, where the design changes from being most modern to most naturalistic as it moves away from the house. After seamlessly transitioning from inside to outside, one immediately encounters the dining terrace adjacent to a glass-block wall. Just beyond, to the southeast, a series of staggered, stone retaining walls—the lowest of which includes an innovative and discrete built-in barbecue—cascades up the sloping landscape, gracefully navigating the dramatic grade differential and creating further grass terraces. This is a truly modern landscape for everyday living.

Borrowing imagery from artists such as Jean Arp, Joan Miró, and Henry Moore, the biomorphic forms of the flagstone terrace recall the shape of an artist's palette and also echo the sensuous forms of the interior curved and cantilevered staircase. Additionally, to the southwest, at the opposite end of the lower terrace, is a shallow, biomorphic concrete pool, which was designed in 1940, a decade before the larger and better-known Dewey Donnell Pool in Sonoma, California. This feature brackets the rectilinear space while enriching the view from the upper terraces, where one can enjoy the inspired forms below.

The two free-form landscape features are knitted together with lawn and connected by a naturalistic flagstone walkway. Moving up the slope, the remaining walls that define the upper terraces seem as appropriate for the modernist home as they do for the regional landscape of the time. Indeed, the tenets of naturalistic design are as evident at the Frank property as they are at Allegheny County's North and South Parks (designed and built from 1927 to 1932) or at the more distant Gropius House in Lincoln, Massachusetts (completed just one year earlier than the Frank House). It is also worth noting that the Pittsburgh-area work—both the Frank House at a residential scale and the North and South Parks designed by local landscape architect Paul B. Riis—bear a resemblance to that of the midwestern landscape architect Jens Jensen. Jensen's designs made use of native species and local, natural materials to construct landscape features, including natural stones for swimming pools and shelters. The same can be said of the walks and walls designed for the Cecelia and Robert Frank property, although their juxtapositions reflect the ideas of Christopher Tunnard, who wrote that "the right style for the twentieth century is no style at all, but a new conception of planning the human environment."[5]

NOTES

1. Joseph Hudnut, "The Modern Garden," in Christopher Tunnard, *Gardens in the Modern Landscape*, 2nd ed. (London: Architectural Press, 1948), 178.

2. Now known as the Alan I W Frank House.

3. Anthony Alofsin, *The Struggle for Modernism: Architecture, Landscape Architecture and City Planning at Harvard* (New York: W.W. Norton, 2002), 11.

4. James C. Rose, "Articulate Form in Landscape Design," *Pencil Points* (February 1939).

5. Christopher Tunnard, "Modern Gardens for Modern Houses: Reflections on Current Trends in Landscape Design," republished in *Modern Landscape Architecture: a Critical Review* (Cambridge, MA: MIT Press, 1993), 159–65. Originally published in *Landscape Architecture* (January 1942).

The Frank House took inspiration from modern art to complement the natural forms the site offered. The result was a landscape conceived to introduce new shapes, materials, and spatial relationships—truly a modernist landscape for everyday living.

Harvard Art Museums, 1940

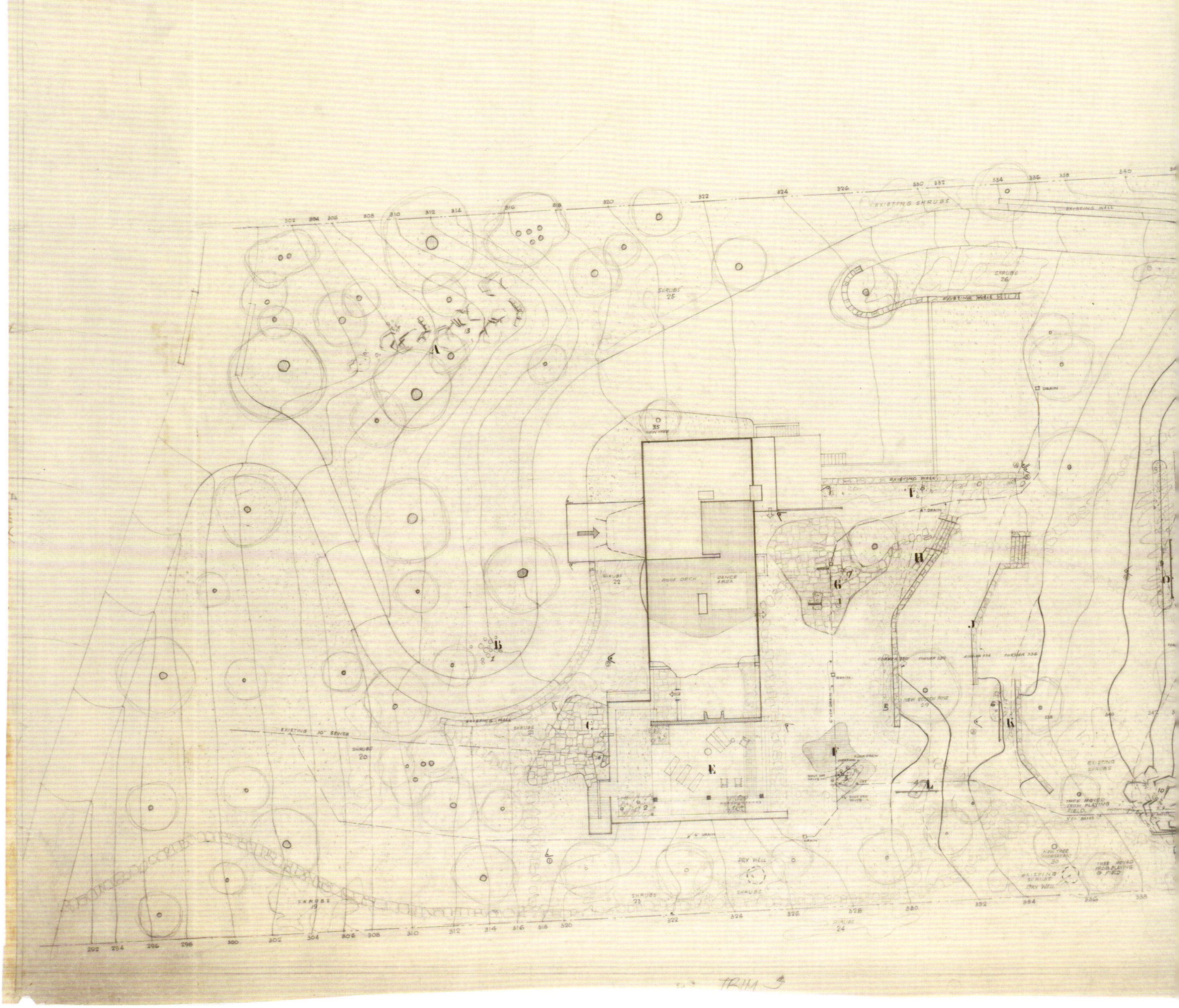

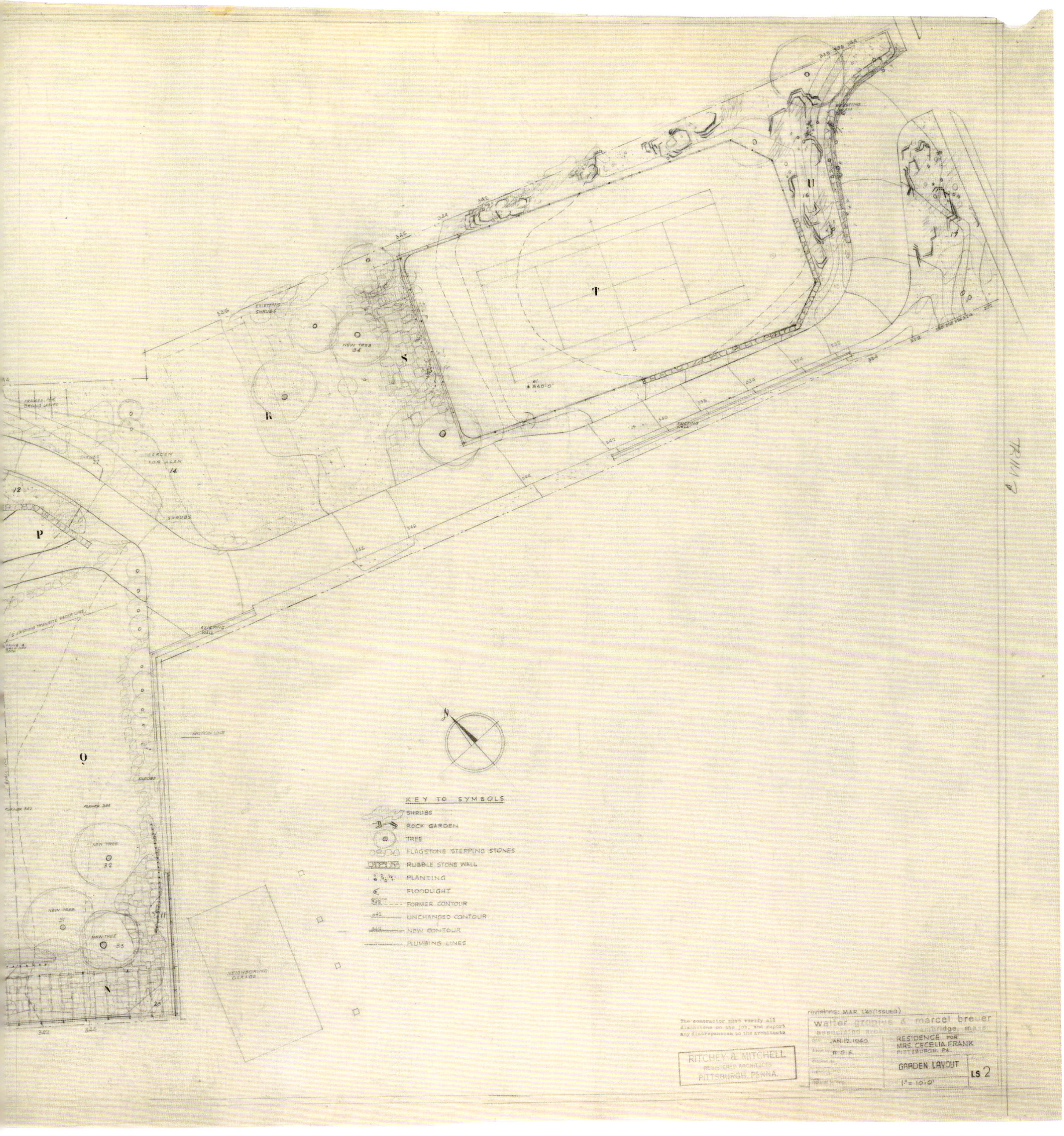

T
S
R
U
P
Q
N
NEW TREE
34
GARDEN FOR ALEN
14
SHRUBS
EXISTING SHRUBS
SECTION LINE
NEW TREE
32
NEW TREE
31
NEW TREE
33
NEIGHBORING GARAGE
KEY TO SYMBOLS
SHRUBS
ROCK GARDEN
TREE
FLAGSTONE STEPPING STONES
RUBBLE STONE WALL
PLANTING
FLOODLIGHT
FORMER CONTOUR
UNCHANGED CONTOUR
NEW CONTOUR
PLUMBING LINES
The contractor must verify all dimensions on the job, and report any discrepancies to the architects
RITCHEY & MITCHELL
REGISTERED ARCHITECTS
PITTSBURGH, PENNA.
revisions: MAR. 1/40 (ISSUED)
walter gropius & marcel breuer
associated architects cambridge, mass.
JAN. 12. 1940
R. G. S.
RESIDENCE FOR
MRS. CECELIA FRANK
PITTSBURGH, PA.
GARDEN LAYOUT
LS 2
1" = 10'-0"

The nature-shaped concrete pool was designed a decade before larger and better-known examples in other parts of the country. This feature completes the space while enriching the view.

Richard Barnes, 2008

Cascades of wisteria.

Alan I W Frank, 2010

Pink dogwood in early spring.

Alan I W Frank, 2010

Red and gold peonies explode in color outside the living room, expressing the exuberant new architecture and spirit that make the Frank House a masterwork.

Alan I W Frank, 2010

ACKNOWLEDGEMENTS

The Foundation wishes to express its profound gratitude to the following people who have helped bring this book to life:

Ken Argentieri and David Chisholm, for their honesty, integrity, and dedication over decades.

Laura Whitby, a long-time friend and Design Director of the Alan I W Frank House Foundation, our longest serving volunteer, having been with us for twelve delightful years.

Bradley Fisher, a long-time friend, for the introduction and captions.

And the many others who have helped over the years including:
AJ, Jay Addleman, Mary-Lou Arscott, Richard Barnes, Wendy Bennett, Barry Bergdoll, Charles Birnbaum, John Block, Susan Block, Claudia Brandenburg, Kenny Brown, Tom Brown, Betsy Burke, Ann Cahouet, Bonnie Cline, Tony Cook, Eric Countryman, Butch Dee, Andy Eller, Glenn Foglio, Kenneth Frampton, Chris Frangiosa, Alice Freer, Robin Freer, Cindy Frischman, Frank Giovannitti, David Graciano, Rick Graciano, Dave Guthrie, Doug Heuck, Scott Izzo, Jade-Snow Joachim, Mike Karwowski, Jim Linz, Alex Marshall, Chris Masaitis, Don McDevitt, Charles Miers, Tom Monfried, Toshiko Mori, Francis Nowalk, Carol Page, Richard Pare, Bill Patrizio, Chuck Queenan, Jenn Rawson, John Rosato, Mike Rothmeyer, Nick Rothmeyer, Nick Rothmeyer Jr, Ray Ryan, Janet Sarbaugh, Kevin Sarver, Tom Schmidt, Kurt Shaw, Dave Sinclair, Joe Skapura, Tim Snyder, Erica Stoller, Ezra Stoller, Louise Sturgess, Al Tannler, Tom Thompson, Jay Turnbull, Marylynn Uricchio, Kelly Vars, Howard Vetter, Lynda Waggoner, Rick Webber, Arthur Ziegler, Ben Zombek.

PHOTOGRAPHY CREDITS

Photo credits can be found with each photo caption. Additional photo credits are listed below.

p. 185: Robert Frank, 1939. Harvard Art Museums

pp. 194–195: Town & Country Magazine, Hearst Magazine Media, Inc.

p. 205: (left) Portrait of architect Walter Gropius. Photography. Berlin. 1955. (Photograph by Imagno/Getty Images); (right) Marcel Breuer at the site of the exhibition, "The House in the Museum Garden." April 12, 1949 through October 30, 1949. The Museum of Modern Art, New York. Gelatin-silver print, 7 1/2 x 9" (19 x 24.1 cm). Photographic Archive. The Museum of Modern Art Archives. Photographer: Homer Page. The Museum of Modern Art Digital Image © The Museum of Modern Art/Licensed by SCALA/ Art Resource, NY. With permission of HOMER PAGE ARCHIVE.

pp. 223, 224, 225: Photographs Courtesy of Sotheby's, Inc. © 2005. Property of Alan I W Frank

pp. 226 (all), 228 (all): Marcel Breuer Papers, Special Collections Research Center, Syracuse University Libraries

pp. 232–233: W.C. Vaughan Co. Archives. E.R. Butler & Co. Research Library

p. 234: Kennedy. Frank Residence, Pittsburgh, Pennsylvania, 1939–1940: Numerals - light signals (full size), 1939–1940 Graphite on paper; 22.5 x 31.5 cm (8 7/8 x 12 3/8 in.) Harvard Art Museums/Busch-Reisinger Museum, Gift of Walter Gropius, BRGA.90.94 Photo: Imaging Department © President and Fellows of Harvard College

p. 237: Kennedy. Frank Residence, Pittsburgh, Pennsylvania, 1939–1940: Suggested shell, Wendel Urn: details (full size), 1939–1940 Graphite on paper; 43.4 x 83.5 cm (17 1/16 x 32 7/8 in.) Harvard Art Museums/Busch-Reisinger Museum, Gift of Walter Gropius, BRGA.90.100 Photo: Imaging Department © President and Fellows of Harvard College

pp. 244–245: Walter Gropius. Frank Residence, Pittsburgh, Pennsylvania, 1939–1940: Landscaping plan, 1939–1940 Graphite with ink on paper; 88.5 x 172 cm (34 13/16 x 67 11/16 in.) Harvard Art Museums/Busch-Reisinger Museum, Gift of Walter Gropius, BRGA.90.244 Photo: Imaging Department © President and Fellows of Harvard College.

Printed in China

ESSAY AUTHORS

ALAN I W FRANK first met Walter Gropius and Marcel Breuer when he was a very young boy, beginning what would become a lifelong enthusiasm for their pioneering work. After graduating from Harvard, Alan received a graduate degree from Columbia University. He served as a U.N. war correspondent during the Korean War and later as a Special Agent of the Counter Intelligence Corps, then turned his talents to his first love: inventing new technology and bringing it to market. Alan holds sixteen patents, and has served as president of National Petroleum and many other corporations. He has also held leadership roles in development and governance for Columbia University, Harvard University, Rensselaer Polytechnic Institute, and Pittsburgh History & Landmarks. Today, as president of the Alan I W Frank House Foundation, Alan oversees the effort to preserve and restore one of the world's most important architectural treasures.

KENNETH FRAMPTON was born in 1930 and trained as an architect at the Architectural Association School of Architecture, London. He has worked as an architect and as an architectural historian and critic, and is now Ware Professor at the Graduate School of Architecture, Planning and Preservation, Columbia University, New York. He has taught at a number of leading institutions in the field, including the Royal College of Art in London, the ETH in Zurich, the Berlage Institute in Amsterdam, EPFL in Lausanne and the Accademia di Architettura in Medrisio. Frampton is the author of numerous essays on modern and contemporary architecture, and has served on many international juries for architectural awards and building commissions. In addition to *Modern Architecture: A Critical History* (1980), his publications include *Studies in Tectonic Culture* (1995), *Labour, Work and Architecture* (2002), *A Genealogy of Modern Architecture: Comparative Critical Analysis of Built Form* (2016) and *Frank Lloyd Wright: Reflections on Culture and Politics 1894-1959* (2017). He was the recipient of the Leone d'Oro at the 2018 Venice Biennale.

BARRY BERGDOLL is Meyer Schapiro Professor of Art History and Archeology at Columbia University, and served as Philip Johnson Chief Curator of Architecture and Design at the Museum of Modern Art, from 2007 to 2014. He has organized, curated, and consulted on landmark exhibitions of nineteenth- and twentieth-century architecture both at MoMA and in Paris. He is author or co-editor of many publications including *Bauhaus 1919-1933: Workshops for Modernity* (MoMA, 2009); *Home Delivery: Fabricating the Modern Dwelling* (MoMA 2008); and *Mies in Berlin* (MoMA 2001), as well as *Karl Friedrich Schinkel: An Architecture for Prussia* (Rizzoli, 1994); *Léon Vaudoyer: Historicism in the Age of Industry* (Architectural History Foundation 1994); and *European Architecture 1750-1890*, in the Oxford History of Art series, 2000. He served as president of the Society of Architectural Historians from 2006 to 2008.

CHARLES A BIRNBAUM, FASLA, is the president, CEO, and founder of The Cultural Landscape Foundation (TCLF). Prior to TCLF, Birnbaum spent fifteen years as the coordinator of the National Park Service Historic Landscape Initiative and a decade in private practice in New York City, with a focus on landscape preservation and urban design. He has conceived and overseen various projects at the Foundation including What's Out There—a searchable database of the nation's designed landscape heritage, and has authored and edited myriad publications, including *Shaping the Postwar Landscape* (2018), the Modern Landscapes: Transition and Transformation series (2012–14), *Shaping the American Landscape* (2009), *Design with Culture* (2005), and *Preserving Modern Landscape Architecture* Volumes I and II (1999, 2004). In 1996, the ASLA inducted Birnbaum as a Fellow of the Society. He served as a Loeb Fellow at Harvard's Graduate School of Design, (1997–98) and in 2004, was awarded the Rome Prize in Historic Preservation and Conservation. He served as Glimcher Distinguished Professor at Ohio State University's Knowlton School of Architecture in 2008, and as a visiting professor at Columbia University Graduate School of Architecture Planning + Preservation (2012–16). The ASLA awarded him three medals: LaGasse Medal (2008), the President's Medal (2009), and the ASLA Medal (2017), the Society's highest award. Birnbaum is a frequent contributor to *The Huffington Post*.